Focusing on
IELTS

Academic
Practice Tests

Focusing on IELTS

Academic
Practice Tests

Second edition

MACMILLAN

Philip Gould
Michael Clutterbuck

First edition published 2004 by the National Centre for English Language Teaching and Research, Macquarie University (reprinted once)
Second edition published 2011 by
MACMILLAN EDUCATION AUSTRALIA PTY LTD
15–19 Claremont Street, South Yarra 3141

Associated companies and representatives
throughout the world.

National Library of Australia
cataloguing in publication data

Author:	Gould, Philip, 1959–
Title:	Focusing on IELTS: Academic Practice Tests / Philip Gould, Michael Clutterbuck.
Edition:	2nd ed.
ISBN:	978 1 4202 3022 2 (pbk.)
Subjects:	International English Language Testing System.
	English language—Study and teaching—Foreign speakers.
	English language—Examinations.
Other authors/contributors:	Clutterbuck, Michael.
Dewey number:	428.007

Publisher: Vivienne Winter
Project editors: Kirstie Innes-Will and Laura Howell
Editor: Ingrid De Baets
Illustrator: Andy Craig and Nives Porcellato
Cover and text designer: Anne Stanhope
Photo research and permissions clearance: Jes Senbergs
Typeset in 11.5 pt Sabon by Marg Jackson, Emtype Desktop Publishing
Cover image: Shutterstock

Printed in China

Contents

How to use this book

There are no magic formulas or secret keys that guarantee a good score in the IELTS test. The best way to prepare for the exam is to gradually improve your overall English listening, reading, writing and speaking abilities.

It is useful to train for the kinds of texts and questions you will face in an IELTS exam. *Focusing on IELTS: Academic Practice Tests* contains complete Reading, Writing, Listening and Speaking practice tests for you to try out. Each test in this book is identical in format to the Academic IELTS tests themselves. You should work through these under test conditions, which means working in a room where you won't be disturbed and only spending an hour on each Reading and Writing Test. There are sample answer sheets at the end of the Listening and Reading units for you to photocopy and use each time you do a practice Listening or Reading Test. This book also contains three recorded Speaking Tests for you to listen to. You can read the transcripts of these Speaking Tests along with an analysis of each of the three candidates' performances. At the back of the book, there are transcripts for the Listening Tests and an answer key for the Listening and Reading Tests. There are sample answers for the Writing Tests.

You can use this book individually as an independent study guide to prepare for the Academic IELTS test or as practice materials for an IELTS preparation course with a teacher.

You may also want to work more intensively on the skills needed in the different sections of the test. For this reason *Focusing on IELTS: Academic Practice Tests* has been written to accompany *Focusing on IELTS: Reading and Writing Skills* by Jeremy Lindeck, Jannette Greenwood and Kerry O'Sullivan (Macmillan 2011) and *Focusing on IELTS: Listening and Speaking Skills* by Steven Thurlow and Kerry O'Sullivan (Macmillan 2011). These two books thoroughly examine the skills you need and teach useful strategies to help you perform well in the test.

Acknowledgments

Author acknowledgments

I would like to thank the following people for their help during the writing of this book: Anna Dash, Alison Babbage, Lisa Barrett, Penny Bell, Mary Cristaudo, Pauline Cullen, Dennis Derkenne, Mary Jane Hogan, Xiaojing Luo, Diana Montgomery, Viv Winter and Hasan Can Yuksel. Thanks also to the students who helped with the trialling of these materials.

Philip Gould

I am grateful for the friendly support I have received from Vivienne Winter at Macmillan, and also for the helpful advice and recommendations from Anna Dash, Kate Chandler and Philip Gould. Ingrid De Baets also made valuable suggestions, and I would like particularly to acknowledge the expert and detailed guidance from Mary Jane Hogan.

Michael Clutterbuck

Publisher acknowledgments

The author and publisher are grateful to the following for permission to reproduce copyright material:

Photographs:

iStockPhoto/René Lorenz, **14**.

Other Material:

Extract from *The Private Life of Plants* by David Attenborough, BBC Books, 1995, **62–3**; Extract from a table of statistics on gross national saving, from Guonan Ma & Wang Yi, *BIS Working Papers No. 132*, 'China's high saving rate: myth and reality', Bank of International Settlements, June 2010. The original publication is available free of charge on the BIS website www.bis.org, **92**; Graph, 'Most important thing contributing to feelings of stress you may have, by age group, 2002', adapted from Statistics Canada publication, *A Portrait of Seniors in Canada*, catalogue 89-519-XIE2006001, at this url address: http://www.statcan.gc.ca/pub/89-519-x/2006001/c-g/4181502-eng.htm, **86**; Extract from article, 'Vines in the Sky,' by Michael Dumiak, *Cosmos*, Issue 18, December 2007/January

2008, 48–9; Extract from article, 'Mass Strandings,' by Cat O'Donovan, *Cosmos*, Issue 30, December 2009/January 2010, 77–8; Extract from article, 'Flying Doctors' by Brian Cross, reproduced with permission, 73–4; Extract from *The History of Clocks*, by Eric Burton, Little, Brown and Co, 2000, 38–9; Extract from article, 'Animal Minds' by Virginia Morell, *National Geographic*, vol. 213, no. 3, March 2008, 44–5; Extract from article, 'The Decline of Angkor Wat' by Richard Stone, *National Geographic*, vol. 216, no. 1, June 2009, 59–60; Extract from article, 'Trash Trackers' by Catherine Brahic, *New Scientist*, vol. 203, no. 2726, 19 September 2009, 42–3; Extract from article, 'Dark Power' by Marcus Chown, *New Scientist*, 28 November 2009, 67–8; Extract from *How Language Works* by David Crystal, Penguin Books, 2006, 54–5; Extract from *How the Stockmarket Really Works* by Leo Gough, Prentice Hall, 2008, 70–1.

What is in the listening module?

This test is the same for Academic and General Training candidates.

Time allowed	Approximately 30 minutes, plus 10 minutes to transfer answers to answer sheet
Procedure	The listening module is the first part of the test you will do. The listening module is recorded using a range of accents of standard English. The recording is played once only. Candidates are given a question booklet. Time is given to read the questions before each section is heard. As you listen to the recording of each section, write your answers in the question booklet. At the end of the fourth section, you are given 10 minutes to transfer your answers to an answer sheet.
Number of questions	40 questions (10 questions per section) 1 mark per question
Structure of the test	**Section 1:** a conversation between two speakers in a normal life situation, e.g. buying a ticket **Section 2:** a monologue (i.e. spoken by one speaker) about a social (non-academic) topic, e.g. joining a club **Section 3:** a conversation between two to four speakers about an educational or training topic, e.g. what the students are studying **Section 4:** a presentation by one speaker in a situation related to educational or training contexts

Summary of the structure	Easier	Section 1	Dialogue	Social topics
	↓	Section 2	Monologue	
		Section 3	Dialogue	Education and training topics
	Harder	Section 4	Monologue	

Listening strategies and skills	See detailed guidelines in 'Listening strategies and skills', *Focusing on IELTS: Listening and Speaking Skills* (Thurlow and O'Sullivan 2011), pages 13–47.

Question types

The following question types are used in the listening module:

▼ *Multiple choice* – you have to choose one answer from three alternatives or two answers from five alternatives.

▼ *Short answer* – you have to answer a question. You will be given a maximum number of words and/or numbers for your answer.

▼ *Sentence completion* – you have to find words that correctly complete a sentence.

▼ *Form/note/summary/flow-chart/table completion* – you have to complete a form, set of notes, summary, flow-chart or table. You will be given a maximum number of words for your answer.

▼ *Labelling a diagram/plan/map* – you have to identify features of a diagram, plan or map.

▼ *Matching* – you have to choose answers from a box containing possible answers.

For detailed explanation, see *Focusing on IELTS: Listening and Speaking Skills* (Thurlow and O'Sullivan 2011) pages 6–12.

Tips for doing the Listening Test

▼ Make sure you are familiar with each question type before you do the test so you know how to respond.

▼ Use the time given to read the questions before each section.

▼ Remember to look at all the sets of questions in each section, not just the first set.

▼ Follow the instructions exactly; for example, regarding the maximum number of words your response should have.

▼ Use the questions to identify the topic of each section and predict what vocabulary you might hear.

▼ Listen with attention to the overall topic so that what you hear makes sense.

▼ Anticipate the type of information needed to answer each question.

▼ Remember that you may hear synonyms and paraphrases of words and ideas in the questions.

▼ Be aware of the question following the one you are answering and move on if you hear the next answer.

▼ Stay focused on the test; don't be distracted or let your attention wander.

▼ If you miss a question, guess an answer in the time given to review your responses.

▼ Be very careful to copy your answers correctly onto the answer sheet.

▼ Be careful with spelling as incorrect spelling is penalised.

Listening Test 1

TIME ALLOWED: APPROXIMATELY 30 MINUTES, PLUS 10 MINUTES TO TRANSFER ANSWERS

NUMBER OF QUESTIONS: 40

This test has been written to simulate the IELTS test in its style, format, level of difficulty, question types and length. You should do this test under IELTS test conditions. This means playing the recording only once without pausing or stopping.

Instructions

You will hear four different recordings and you will have to answer questions on what you hear.

There will be time for you to read the instructions and questions before the recording is played. You will also have the opportunity to check your answers.

The recording will be played **ONCE** only.

The test is in four sections. Write your answers on the question sheet as you listen. At the end of Section 4 you have 10 minutes to transfer your answers onto the answer sheet, which is on page 31. When you finish, check the answer key at the back of the book.

Now turn to Section 1 on the next page.

SECTION 1

Questions 1–5

Complete the notes below.

CD 1 • Track 2

*Write **NO MORE THAN THREE WORDS AND/OR A NUMBER** for each answer.*

Change of address	
Customer number:	Example: ...**5062 7840**..
Name:	**1** ....
Date of birth:	**2** ....
New address:	18 King Street, **3** ....
New telephone number:	**4** ....
Billing period:	**5** ....

Questions 6–10

*Choose the correct letter, **A**, **B** or **C**.*

6 The contract the customer has now is

  A Economy Saver.

  B Flexible Bundle.

  C Home Plus.

7 The contract the customer will have in the future is

  A Economy Saver.

  B Home Plus.

  C Three-In-One.

8 There are no limits on Internet downloads in the period from

  A 10 pm to 6 am.

  B 1 am to 6 am.

  C 11 pm to 2 am.

9 Most of the phone calls this customer makes are

  A to friends.

  B to relatives.

  C for work.

10 Overall, the customer finds that the service of the telephone company is

  A satisfactory.

  B excellent.

  C very good.

SECTION 2

Questions 11–17

Complete the notes below.

*Write **NO MORE THAN THREE WORDS AND/OR A NUMBER** for each answer.*

▼   Always wear **11** .... inside the hotel.

▼   Hire beach items at the **12** ....

▼   Reception opening hours **13** ....

▼   Linen and towels are changed **14** ....

▼   Smoking allowed only **15** ....

▼   Do not feed the **16** .... and the ....

▼   Be quiet after **17** ....

Questions 18–20

*Choose **TWO** letters, A–E.*

18   Which TWO types of rubbish are *not* recycled?

    A   food scraps

    B   glass

    C   metal

    D   newspaper

    E   plastic

19   Which TWO types of facilities in the hotel do you have to pay to use?

    A   gym

    B   spa

    C   billiards

    D   Internet

    E   DVDs

20   What are TWO places for evening entertainment within walking distance of the hotel?

    A   bar

    B   casino

    C   cinema

    D   karaoke club

    E   nightclub

Questions 21–26

When patients have the following problems, who does the nurse need to contact first?

Choose your answers from the box and write the correct letters, A–F, next to questions 21–26.

A confusion	**D** poor eyesight
B instability when walking	**E** refusal to accept help
C pets as a risk factor	**F** weakness

21	physiotherapist	....
22	doctor	....
23	occupational therapist	....
24	aged care team	....
25	dietitian	....
26	falls clinic	....

Questions 27–30

Choose the correct letter, A, B or C.

27 In which of the following medical problems can the damage be reversed?

    A long-term, excessive alcohol consumption

    B Pick's disease

    C a brain tumour

28 Anxiety is a common symptom among people with dementia due to

    A side effects of medication.

    B frustration and suspicion.

    C fear of the future.

29 People with dementia tend to enjoy food that is

    A sweet.

    B easy to chew.

    C salty.

30 Recent research has shown people with dementia often benefit from

    A singing.

    B listening to music.

    C exercise.

SECTION 4

Questions 31–36

Questions 31–40

Complete the notes below.

*Write **NO MORE THAN TWO WORDS AND/OR A NUMBER** for each answer.*

The Tuareg

▼ Difficult to count Tuareg population due to **31** …………….……………. .

▼ Tuareg people's skin often looks blue because of colour of their **32** …………….…………. .

Diet

▼ Dry season: grains and fruit.

▼ Wet season: **33** …………….…………… and …………….……………. .

Occupations of Tuareg in countryside

▼ Breeding animals.

▼ Trade and **34** …………….…………… .

Camel caravans

▼ For trade between Sahel and Mediterranean.

▼ Maximum load per camel: 300 kilograms plus rider.

▼ Travel south slowly at first so camels can **35** …………….…………… .

Trade partners

▼ Hausa people trade cloth and millet for **36** …………….…………… and dates.

Questions 37–40

Choose the correct letter, A, B or C.

37   The main work of Tuareg women in growing crops is

    A   planting.

    B   irrigating.

    C   harvesting.

38   Tuareg women mainly look after

    A   camels and cattle.

    B   cattle and sheep.

    C   goats and donkeys.

39   Salt prices are highest in the hotter weather because at that time of year

    A   animals need more salt.

    B   the quality of the salt is best.

    C   transport by camel is more difficult.

40   Craftsmen had low status in traditional Tuareg society because

    A   they did not work as farmers.

    B   they did not live as nomads.

    C   they had a different attitude to education.

Listening Test 2

TIME ALLOWED: APPROXIMATELY 30 MINUTES, PLUS 10 MINUTES TO TRANSFER ANSWERS

NUMBER OF QUESTIONS: 40

This test has been written to simulate the IELTS test in its style, format, level of difficulty, question types and length. You should do this test under IELTS test conditions. This means playing the recording only once without pausing or stopping.

Instructions

You will hear four different recordings and you will have to answer questions on what you hear.

There will be time for you to read the instructions and questions before the recording is played. You will also have the opportunity to check your answers.

The recording will be played **ONCE** only.

The test is in four sections. Write your answers on the question sheet as you listen. At the end of Section 4 you have 10 minutes to transfer your answers onto the answer sheet, which is on page 31. When you finish, check the answer key at the back of the book.

Now turn to Section 1 on the next page.

LISTENING

Complete the notes below.

*Write **NO MORE THAN TWO WORDS AND/OR A NUMBER** for each answer.*

Application for driving licence	
Name:	Example: *Theresa Collins* ....
Class of licence:	1 ....
Date of birth:	17 March 1994
Address:	2 .... Street, Bentley
Phone number:	3 ....
Identification:	4 ....
Method of payment:	5 ....

Questions 6–10

*Choose the correct letter, **A**, **B** or **C**.*

6   In the test of road rules, you are allowed to make no more than

    A   one mistake.

    B   two mistakes.

    C   four mistakes.

7   A person who has a learner's licence can only drive with a person

    A   who has a provisional licence.

    B   who has a full licence.

    C   who is an authorised driving instructor.

8   A provisional licence is valid for

    A   9 months.

    B   18 months.

    C   6 months.

9   The maximum speed for a person who has a learner's licence is

    A   60 km per hour.

    B   100 km per hour.

    C   80 km per hour.

10   While driving, a person is

    A   not allowed to use a mobile phone.

    B   only allowed to use a mobile phone if they are not holding it.

    C   allowed to send an SMS.

SECTION 2   QUESTIONS 11–20

Questions 11–15

What is stated about the following means of transport from the airport?

*Choose your answers from the box below and write the correct letters, **A–G**, next to questions 11–15.*

A cheapest	**E** most popular
B fastest	**F** most reliable
C most comfortable	**G** safest
D most environmentally friendly	

11   trains   ....

12   minibuses   ....

13   buses   ....

14   cars   ....

15   taxis   ....

Questions 16–20

Label the floor plan below.

*Choose **FIVE** answers from the box below and write the correct letters, **A–H**, next to numbers 16–20 on the floor plan.*

A cafe	**E** pharmacy
B dress shop	**F** smoking room
C Internet cafe	**G** toilets
D newsagency	**H** wine bar

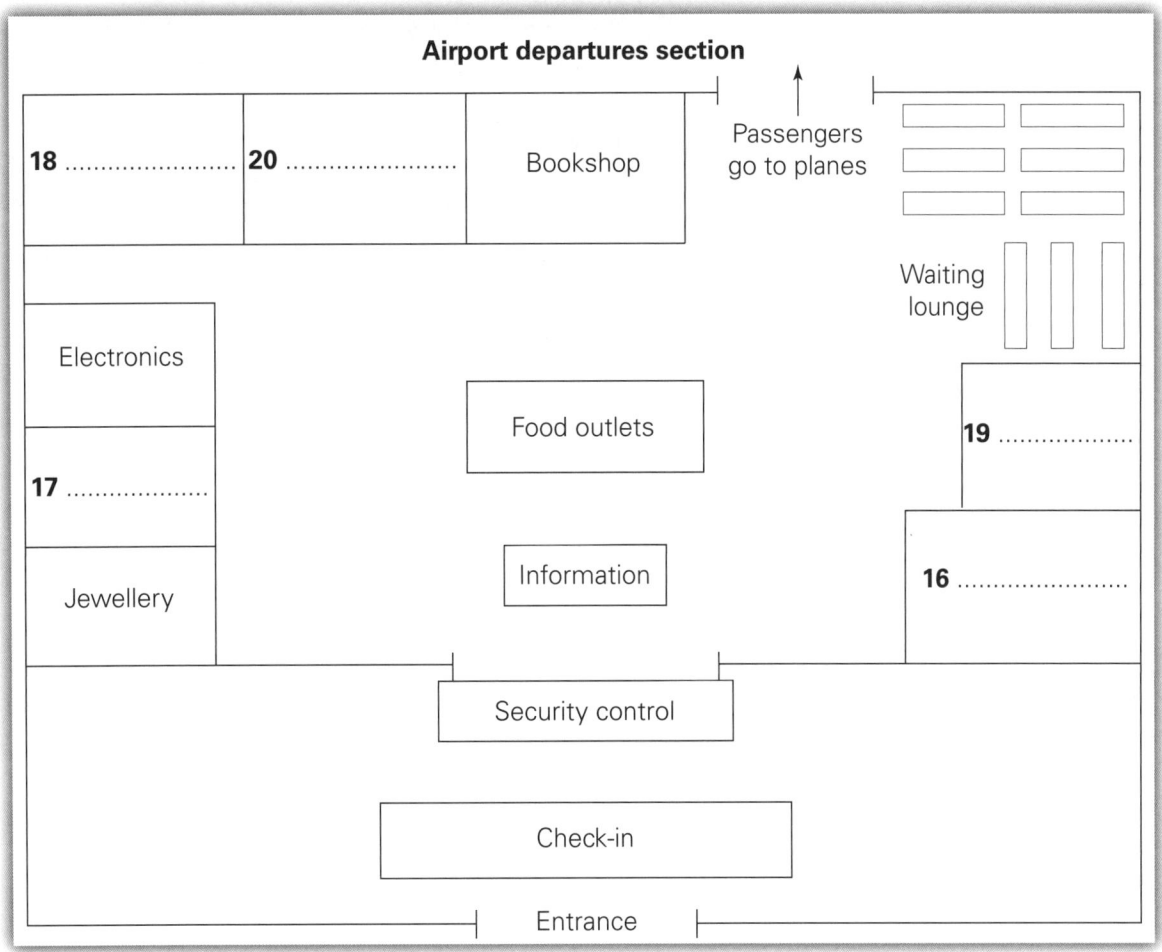

Airport departures section

18	20	Bookshop	Passengers go to planes ↑

Waiting lounge

Electronics

17 ....

Jewellery

Food outlets

Information

19 ....

16 ....

Security control

Check-in

Entrance

SECTION 3

Questions 21–26

Choose the correct letter, A, B or C.

21 The largest numbers of Tasmanian devils live in

    A   coastal areas.

    B   drier forests.

    C   rainforests.

22 An adult female can weigh up to

    A   4.5 kg.

    B   9 kg.

    C   13 kg.

23 Tasmanian devils are

    A   shy.

    B   aggressive.

    C   friendly.

24 In one year an adult female usually raises

    A   one baby.

    B   three babies.

    C   twenty babies.

25 Tasmanian devils become independent when they are about

    A   5 months old.

    B   8 months old.

    C   2 years old.

26 Farmers are

    A   permitted to shoot or poison them.

    B   paid to kill them.

    C   prohibited from killing them.

Questions 27–30

Complete the summary below using words from the box.

*Choose **FOUR** answers from the box and write the correct letters, **A–I**, next to questions 27–30.*

A bark	**F** friendly
B bite	**G** sick
C clean	**H** yawn
D dead	**I** young
E fight	

Tasmanian devils live alone and move slowly. They usually eat **27** .... animals and

are not affected by the diseases of the animals they eat. They are generally **28** ....

They travel long distances at night and are famous for their strong appetite. To decide the order

in which they eat, Tasmanian devils often **29** .... , whereas if they are afraid, they

30 ....

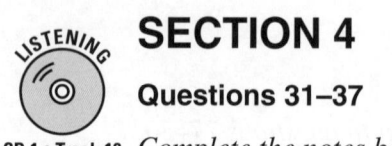
SECTION 4

Questions 31–37

Complete the notes below.

*Write **NO MORE THAN TWO WORDS AND/OR A NUMBER** for each answer.*

Framework of survey

▼ Aims of survey: investigate type of people who do yoga, styles of yoga, frequency of

practice, **31** .... for practice, benefits of yoga.

▼ Conducted via Internet due to effectiveness and **32** ....

▼ 4,000 respondents nationwide.

▼ Respondents: one-third teachers, two-thirds students, **33** .... women.

Findings of survey

▼ Males and younger people prefer more vigorous styles.

▼ Uses of yoga: **34** .... and .... , meditation,

spiritual path.

▼ Approximately 2% of total population practise yoga; highest participation 35- to

44-year-olds.

▼ Less time spent on physical exercise due to rise in popularity of **35** ....

▼ 56% of yoga students do yoga one to two times per week; 56% of yoga teachers do yoga

five to seven times per week.

▼ Reasons for starting yoga practice: health and fitness, **36** .... , treat

physical problem.

▼ Major motivation to continue yoga: **37** ....

Questions 38–40

Choose the correct letter, A, B or C.

38 A major cause of injuries when doing yoga is

    A   headstand and shoulder stand.

    B   students causing injuries to themselves.

    C   teachers pushing students too hard.

39 A typical yoga teacher earns money

    A   only from teaching yoga.

    B   from massage therapy.

    C   from nursing.

40 The speaker concludes that

    A   teaching yoga is not a good way to earn a high income.

    B   yoga is a relatively expensive form of exercise.

    C   the benefits of yoga are uproven.

Listening Test 3

TIME ALLOWED: APPROXIMATELY 30 MINUTES, PLUS 10 MINUTES TO TRANSFER ANSWERS

NUMBER OF QUESTIONS: 40

This test has been written to simulate the IELTS test in its style, format, level of difficulty, question types and length. You should do this test under IELTS test conditions. This means playing the recording only once without pausing or stopping.

Instructions

You will hear four different recordings and you will have to answer questions on what you hear.

There will be time for you to read the instructions and questions before the recording is played. You will also have the opportunity to check your answers.

The recording will be played **ONCE** only.

The test is in four sections. Write your answers on the question sheet as you listen. At the end of Section 4 you have 10 minutes to transfer your answers onto the answer sheet, which is on page 31. When you finish, check the answer key at the back of the book.

Now turn to Section 1 on the next page.

SECTION 1   Questions 1–10

Questions 1–4

Complete the notes below.

*Write **NO MORE THAN TWO WORDS AND/OR A NUMBER** for each answer.*

Details of job applicant	
Name of applicant:	George Peters
Phone number:	Example: *0438 637 935*
Position applied for:	**1** ....
Previous work experience:	worked as a **2** ....
Qualifications:	currently studying **3** ....
Foreign languages spoken:	**4** .... and ....

Questions 5–7

Which duties are part of the job that the man is applying for?

*Choose **THREE** from the list below and write the correct letters, **A–G**, next to questions 5–7.*

A change light bulbs	**E** take food orders
B clear away plates	**F** take luggage to rooms
C deliver morning papers	**G** work in hotel bar
D stock refrigerators	

5 ....

6 ....

7 ....

Questions 8–10

Which of the following are provided for staff by the hotel?

*Choose **THREE** from the list below and write the correct letters, **A–G**, next to questions 8–10.*

A laundry	**E** training
B meals	**F** transport costs
C medical insurance	**G** uniforms
D parking	

8   ....

9   ....

10   ....

CD 2 • Track 3

Questions 11–12

*Choose **TWO** correct letters, A–E.*

11 Which TWO types of visa does the Atwood Immigration office handle?

    A employment

    B medical

    C resident

    D student

    E tourist

12 Which TWO matters do students have to tell the Immigration Department about?

    A change of address

    B change of college

    C holidays

    D marriage

    E work

Questions 13–20

Complete the notes in the flow-chart below.

*Write **NO MORE THAN THREE WORDS AND/OR A NUMBER** for each answer.*

How to extend a student visa

Pay for new course for a minimum period of **13** ....

↓

Letter from college stating that you attended at least **14** .... of previous classes.

↓

Get Form 726C from Immigration: from office or **15** ....

↓

Bank statement showing minimum bank balance of **16** ....

↓

Three **17** ....

↓

Take all documents and passport to Dept of Immigration at least three weeks before expiry of visa.

↓

Pay **18** .... to extend visa.

↓

Wait twelve **19** .... for reply.

↓

Might need to have an **20** ....

Questions 21–24

Choose the correct letter, A, B or C.

21   The annual value of the beauty industry worldwide is

   A $15 billion.

   B $38 billion.

   C $160 billion.

22   The annual growth rate of the global beauty market is

   A   7 per cent.

   B   14 per cent.

   C   40 per cent.

23   The most common form of cosmetic procedure is for

   A   fat.

   B   wrinkles.

   C   teeth.

24   Demand for beauty products increased in the early 20th century due to

   A   packaging.

   B   scientific progress.

   C   photography.

Questions 25–30

Who agrees with the following opinions?

Choose your answers from the box and write the correct letters, A–C, next to questions 25–30.

You may use any answer more than once.

   A Maggie (the female student)
   B Mike (the male student)
   C Maggie and Mike (both students)

---

25   Fifty per cent of the money used for marketing is used effectively.   ....

26   The beauty industry is based on hope and fear.   ....

27   People who are more attractive earn higher incomes.   ....

28   Attractive people tend not to accept poor treatment.   ....

29   Clear skin is seen as a sign of women's youth and health.   ....

30   The current beauty industry promotes fitness.   ....

Questions 31–35

Which of the following sources gave scientists information about the Iceman?

*Choose your answers from the box and write the correct letters, **A–H**, next to questions 31–35.*

A back	**C** fingernail	**E** intestines	**G** stomach
B bones	**D** hair	**F** skin	**H** teeth

31	age when he died	....
32	where he lived	....
33	food normally eaten	....
34	health	....
35	time of year when he died	....

Questions 36–40

*Choose the correct letter, **A**, **B** or **C**.*

36 Moss was used in the Iceman's region

  A   to wrap food.

  B   as toilet paper.

  C   to cook food.

37 His shoes were made from

  A   grass and bark.

  B   deer hide and goat hide.

  C   bearskin and goatskin.

38 It is most likely that the Iceman was a

  A   shepherd.

  B   hunter.

  C   trader.

39 It is now believed the Iceman died

  A   near the rock where his body was found.

  B   while trapped under a rock.

  C   while sleeping on the rock where his body was found.

40 Much evidence was destroyed

  A   due to the manner in which he died and the isolated location of his corpse.

  B   because people initially didn't realise the importance of the discovery.

  C   when the autopsy was carried out to determine the cause of death.

Listening Test 4

TIME ALLOWED: APPROXIMATELY 30 MINUTES, PLUS 10 MINUTES TO TRANSFER ANSWERS

NUMBER OF QUESTIONS: 40

This test has been written to simulate the IELTS test in its style, format, level of difficulty, question types and length. You should do this test under IELTS test conditions. This means playing the recording only once without pausing or stopping.

Instructions

You will hear four different recordings and you will have to answer questions on what you hear.

There will be time for you to read the instructions and questions before the recording is played. You will also have the opportunity to check your answers.

The recording will be played **ONCE** only.

The test is in four sections. Write your answers on the question sheet as you listen. At the end of Section 4 you have 10 minutes to transfer your answers onto the answer sheet, which is on page 31. When you finish, check the answer key at the back of the book.

Now turn to Section 1 on the next page.

SECTION 1

Questions 1–6

Questions 1–10

Label the floor plan below.

Choose FIVE answers from the floor plan and write the correct letters, A–I, next to questions 1–6.

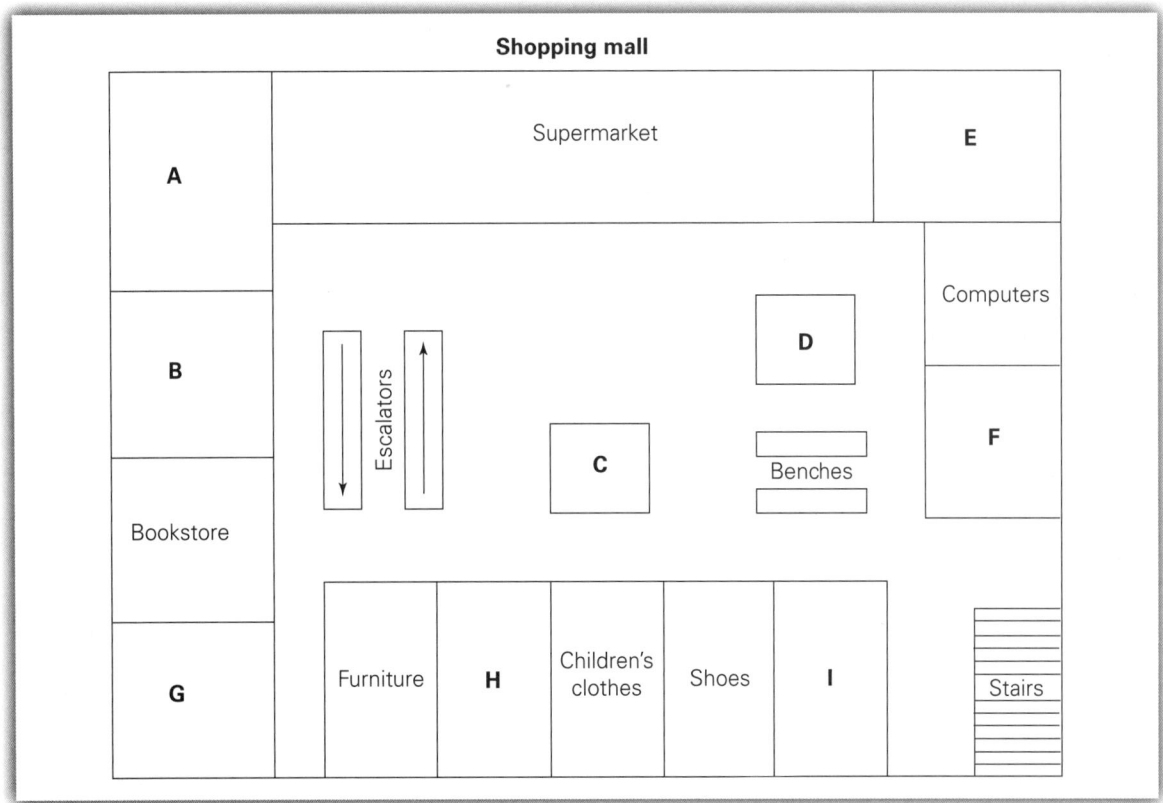

Shopping mall

Supermarket

E

A

Computers

B

D

Escalators

F

C

Benches

Bookstore

G

Furniture | H | Children's clothes | Shoes | I

Stairs

Example

information desk   C

1   children's play centre   ....

2   hairdresser   ....

3   toy store   ....

4   toilets   ....

5   phone kiosk   ....

6   elevator   ....

Questions 7–10

Answer the questions below.

Write **NO MORE THAN TWO WORDS AND/OR A NUMBER** *for each answer.*

7   How much does it cost to leave your car in the car park for four hours? ....

8   What is the minimum age for children at the children's play centre? ....

9   Which level is the food court located on? ....

10 What is located on the top floor of the building? ....

Complete the notes below.

*Write **NO MORE THAN TWO WORDS AND/OR A NUMBER** for each answer.*

The agency

▼   Contented Homes agency began in **11** ………………...………………. .

▼   Agency does most work using the **12** ………………...………………. .

How the system operates

▼   Minimum time period for housesitting is **13** ………………...………………. .

▼   Housesitters do not pay **14** ………………...………………. .

▼   Homeowners check **15** ………………...………………. of housesitters.

▼   Housesitters have fewer **16** ………………...………………. than normal tenants.

Advantages of having housesitters

▼   Prevent **17** ………………...………………. .

▼   Keep your home clean.

▼   Take care of your **18** ………………...………………. and ………………...………………. .

Charges

▼   Agency charges housesitters **19** ………………...………………. to register.

▼   Agency recommends that homeowners organise **20** ………………...………………. .

SECTION 3

Questions 21–25

Where did a majority of the nationalities listed below settle?

*Choose your answer from the box and write the correct letters, **A–C**, next to questions 21–25.*

You may use any answer more than once.

Questions 21–30

> **A** Melbourne
> **B** Sydney
> **C** Other places in Australia

21	British	....
22	Chinese	....
23	Lebanese	....
24	Malaysians	....
25	New Zealanders	....

Questions 26–30

Choose the correct letter, A, B or C.

26   Most migrants chose where to live based on

    A   employment.

    B   community.

    C   real estate.

27   There is a trend for people born in Australia to leave Sydney

    A   because it's becoming too busy and crowded.

    B   due to the inadequate infrastructure.

    C   so they can have more money in retirement.

28   Among people who recently migrated to Australia, the percentage who settled in Sydney and Melbourne was

    A   40%.

    B   50%.

    C   60%.

29   The government is considering encouraging migrants to settle in other areas by

    A   offering tax incentives to employers.

    B   making it easier for farmers to immigrate.

    C   employing people outside Sydney and Melbourne.

30   The number of migrants living in Sydney is likely to be

    A   higher than the statistics indicate.

    B   lower than the statistics indicate.

    C   the same as the statistics indicate.

Complete the table below.

*Write **NO MORE THAN THREE WORDS AND/OR A NUMBER** for each answer.*

Product	Traditional source	Advantages of using hemp
Paper	wood	▼ ready to harvest in **31** .... ▼ no need for **32** ....
Clothing	cotton	▼ needs less **33** .... , fertiliser and pesticides ▼ provides better protection for people against **34** ....
Lamps	**35**	▼ causes less smell
Cars	metal	▼ is **36** .... ▼ decomposes sooner
Fuel	petrol	▼ causes less **37** ....

Questions 38–40

Complete the summary below.

*Choose your answers from the box and write the correct letters, **A–G**, next to questions 38–40.*

A dry	**E** non-toxic
B cheese	**F** shady
C flour	**G** versatile
D long-lasting	

Hemp can be a source of foods and health products. It can produce **38** ....

containing a higher level of protein. It has many applications in the home. Paint made from

hemp is **39** .... Hemp grows well under **40** .... conditions. It is an

environmentally friendly solution to many problems.

LISTENING ANSWER SHEET

Pencil must be used to complete this sheet.

1		
2		
3		
4		
5		
6		
7		
8		
9		
10		
11		
12		
13		
14		
15		
16		
17		
18		
19		
20		

21		
22		
23		
24		
25		
26		
27		
28		
29		
30		
31		
32		
33		
34		
35		
36		
37		
38		
39		
40		
	Total	

This page may be photocopied by the original purchaser.

What is in the reading module?

Format of the test	There are three reading passages of between 700 and 950 words each. The questions require candidates to find information from the passages, and one of the passages may need interpretation of the writer's opinions.
Number of questions	40 questions, 1 mark per question Each section contains 12 to 14 questions.
Time allowed	60 minutes Candidates are recommended to spend approximately 20 minutes on each reading passage.
Reading strategies and skills	See detailed guidelines in 'Reading strategies and skills', *Focusing on IELTS: Reading and Writing Skills* (Lindeck, Greenwood and O'Sullivan 2011), pages 29–84.

Question types

The following question types are used in the reading module:

▼ *Multiple choice* – you have to choose one correct answer to a question from four options, or two or three correct options from a set of five or seven.

▼ *Identifying information* – you have to decide whether a statement is true or false according to the information in the passage, or whether no information about the statement is given.

▼ *Identifying writer's views or claims* – you choose 'yes' if a statement agrees with the opinions or claims of the writer, 'no' if the statement contradicts the writer's opinion or argument, or 'not given' if the passage gives no information on what the writer thinks about the statement.

▼ *Matching information* – you have to match the information stated in each question with the relevant paragraph or section in the passage where the information can be found.

▼ *Matching headings* – you have to select the correct heading from the box to match the main idea of each paragraph or section in the passage.

▼ *Matching features* – from a set of possible options, you have to select the correct option that matches the features or characteristics described in each question.

▼ *Matching sentence endings* – you have to choose the correct option from a list in a box to complete a sentence that reflects information given in the passage.

▼ *Sentence completion* – you have to find a word or phrase in the passage that correctly completes a sentence. You may have to write one, two or three words and/or a number.

▼ *Summary/notes/flow-chart/table completion* – you have to either find words or phrases from the text or select words from a box of possible answers to complete a summary or notes of part of the passage, or a table or flow-chart that represents information in the passage. You may have to write one, two or three words and/or a number.

▼ *Diagram label completion* – you have to find words or phrases from the passage to label the parts of a diagram that reflects information in the passage. You may have to write one, two or three words and/or a number.

▼ *Short-answer questions* – you have to write one, two or three words and/or a number to answer brief questions about information in the passage.

In some question types (for example, *identifying information*) the questions follow the same order in which the information occurs in the passage; in other question types (for example, *matching information*), the answers might be located anywhere in the text or texts.

For detailed explanation, see *Focusing on IELTS: Reading and Writing Skills* (Lindeck, Greenwood and O'Sullivan 2011) pages 5–28.

Tips for doing the Reading Test

▼ Make sure you are familiar with each question type so you know what you have to do.

▼ Remember to keep an eye on the time and make sure you have enough time to do all three sections.

▼ If you cannot answer a question after about a minute, move on to the next question and come back later if you have time.

▼ If you cannot answer a question at all, it is better to guess than to leave a blank.

▼ Leave a few minutes at the end of the test to review your answers.

▼ Check for spelling and grammar in items such as short-answer questions; incorrectly spelled words are penalised.

▼ Check that your response matches the word restrictions given in the instructions (one, two or three words and/or a number).

▼ Take care to write your answers in the correct box on the Answer sheet; a correct answer in the wrong box will be marked as incorrect.

▼ Read quickly through each text or set of texts before you look at the questions to get a general idea of the type of information they contain.

▼ In each question, underline the key word that indicates the information you are looking for.

▼ Remember to use the reading skills of skimming for general ideas and scanning for specific information.

▼ Recognise which questions need you to read carefully for concepts (for example, *matching information*) and which require scanning for details (for example, *table completion*).

▼ Remember to look for synonyms and paraphrases of words and ideas in the questions as well as the exact words.

Reading Test 1

ALL ANSWERS MUST BE WRITTEN ON THE ANSWER SHEET.

The test is divided as follows:

Reading Passage 1   Questions 1 to 13

Reading Passage 2   Questions 14 to 27

Reading Passage 3   Questions 28 to 40

Start at the beginning of the test and work through it. You should answer all the questions. If you cannot do a particular question leave it and go on to the next one. You can return to it later.

TIME ALLOWED: 60 MINUTES

NUMBER OF QUESTIONS: 40

READING PASSAGE 1

You should spend about 20 minutes on questions 1–13.

Domestic clocks

The domestic clock was not exactly invented; it was probably a spin-off from the scientific activities of churchmen, astrologers and mechanics of the Middle Ages interested in increasing their knowledge of the stars or improving discipline in religious communities. Perhaps some 13th-century king or bishop first had a clock in his house as a symbol of prestige or wealth, or perhaps from interest, or to call him to prayer. Certainly, the church assistant needed to know when to warn the watchman to ring the bell in the watchtower to warn the local people about some communal activity such as digging a ditch, preparing to defend themselves against raiders, or gathering to help put a fire out.

So possibly it was the watchman's clock on the wall that became the domestic iron clock of the medieval household. It was a valuable possession, and when the family moved it went with them, just as did any glass windows they had. Iron clocks and lantern clocks, hanging on the wall from a hook, were the first general domestic clocks. The weights that powered them hung below them and generally had to be pulled up twice a day. In some countries, it became fashionable to fit ornate wooden cases around them and mount these clocks on wooden brackets.

Although the weight-driven clock was not originally designed for domestic use, the spring-driven one undoubtedly was. The use of a coiled spring instead of a weight to provide power made possible first the portable clock and subsequently the smaller, personal clock, which was later called a watch. Spring clocks were first made in France in the 1400s, it seems, but little is known of their origin. The earliest spring-driven clock known is dated about 1450. It is like the weight-driven clock of the time but with the weights replaced by coiled springs.

The changeover from weight-driven to spring-driven clocks did not prove so simple, however, because, unlike the falling weight, the coiled spring did not provide a constant source of power. When wound up, the spring gave a force that was very strong, but only for a short time. The force then decreased unevenly for some hours before slowing rapidly. The middle of the range was most useful for driving the clock, but the reducing force was a problem. Early coiled springs also suffered from the fact that they could not be made very evenly or smoothly and did not coil accurately. When this happened, the power was released in uneven bursts. The means adopted to overcome these disadvantages, which directly affected timekeeping accuracy, were twofold.

The first step was to limit the use of the spring to the middle of its action to prevent it from driving the clock when it was too tightly wound up or not wound up tightly enough. The next step was to provide a form of gearing between the spring and the clock to make the power output more even. The method was so simple, ingenious and elegant that it has remained in use, at least in certain types of clock, from the time it was invented until today.

It is called the fusee, meaning a spindle wound with a thread. A fusee is a trumpet-shaped object with a toothed or gear wheel at the larger end, which is connected to the driving wheel of the clock. The trumpet-shaped part has a spiral groove cut in it, and a strong thread attached to the groove at the larger end. The rest of the thread is wound round the barrel of the clock, containing the spring. When the fusee is turned with a key, the thread is pulled off the barrel, which winds up the spring inside it. The thread is wound on the fusee groove, which becomes smaller and smaller in diameter, so that in effect it means the spring drives the clock at a constant speed.

Fusees were used from the 1400s to the early 1900s. This relatively simple device to improve timekeeping by equalising the uneven pull of the mainspring achieved its purpose effectively. Granville Baillie, a leading clockmaker and watchmaker in the 1900s, said of the fusee, 'Perhaps no problem in mechanics has ever been solved so simply and so perfectly.'

Questions 1–5

Do the following statements agree with the information given in Reading Passage 1?

In boxes 1–5 on your answer sheet write

TRUE	if the statement agrees with the information
FALSE	if the statement contradicts the information
NOT GIVEN	if there is no information on this

1   The earliest domestic clocks were developed to provide routine for householders.

2   Medieval clocks remained on the property when the owners sold their home.

3   Pulling the weights on wall-mounted clocks required precise skill.

4   It is the spring inside that allows a watch to be moved around.

5   The first spring-driven clocks had difficulty keeping the correct time.

Questions 6–10

Complete the notes below.

*Choose **NO MORE THAN THREE WORDS** from the passage for each answer.*

Write your answers in boxes 6–10 on your answer sheet.

Early domestic clocks

Weight-driven clocks

▼   Made of **6** ....

▼   Decorated clock cases fixed to the wall with **7** ....

Spring-driven clocks

▼   Location where first produced: **8** ....

▼   Problems keeping **9** .... even

Questions 10–13

Answer the questions below.

*Choose **NO MORE THAN THREE WORDS** from the passage for each answer.*

Write your answers in boxes 10–13 on your answer sheet.

10   What does a fusee look like?

11   What is connected to the spiral groove on a fusee?

12   What object is required to wind the spring on the fusee?

13   What does the gradual reduction of the fusee groove ensure?

READING PASSAGE 2

You should spend about 20 minutes on questions 14–27.

Questions 14–21

Reading Passage 2 has eight paragraphs, **A–H**.

Choose the correct heading for each paragraph from the list of headings below.

*Write the correct number, **i–xi**, in boxes 14–21 on your answer sheet.*

List of headings

i	A lack of information about what is in trash
ii	A change in public attitude
iii	The uncertainty of trash destination
iv	A typical householder's present action
v	Formulating the ultimate rubbish solution
vi	Selection of recycling centres
vii	A way to trace what happens to rubbish
viii	Details of how the research will be done
ix	Variations in the effect of waste on the surrounding area
x	Future sources of useful materials
xi	Network coverage for telecommunications

---

14 Paragraph A

15 Paragraph B

16 Paragraph C

17 Paragraph D

18 Paragraph E

19 Paragraph F

20 Paragraph G

21 Paragraph H

Trash trackers

A So you carefully separate your cardboard from your used glass containers, wash your empty tins and tear the staples off scrap paper. You fill your various bins and put them out to be taken away with the remains of the week's meals and domestic rubbish. And then, safe in the knowledge that you have done your bit for the environment, you forget all about it.

B In fact, the life story of your weekly garbage is just beginning. An aluminium can, for instance, could have a variety of fates. It might be crushed and sent back to the canning factory to be turned into new cans. Or it could end up in the nearest landfill site or get shipped off overseas to be either recycled or dumped. The truth is that nobody can be sure where an individual piece of rubbish will end up or how the junk in the landfill got there.

C New research is planning to find out. In a pilot project, a team from the Massachusetts Institute of Technology (MIT) together with members of the *New Scientist* journal tracked 60 pieces of trash in Seattle in the United States. The next phase of the experiment will begin – 1,000 more pieces of garbage will be electronically tagged and thrown away in New York, Seattle and London, and tracked for two months.

D The experiment is more than just an attempt to satisfy curiosity as to where trash ends up. The idea is to help plan for an ideal world of waste disposal, where nearly everything gets recycled or reused and materials are not sent to landfill faster than the planet is able to produce them.

E At present, that ideal world is a distant dream only. Part of the problem is that we do not know what we are dealing with. While a lot of effort has gone into creating green supply chains to bring products to customers, almost nothing is known about what happens to the waste. This waste is monitored, of course, but only to see how many tonnes of different kinds of garbage arrive at a sorting centre, landfill or incinerator, and how many leave. These are counted as electronic or household waste; the mass is measured, but not in terms of the content.

F In terms of environmental impact, it is the content, not the number of tonnes, that matters. Within the harmless-sounding category of 'household waste', for example, lies everything from carrot peelings to used babies' nappies and low-energy light bulbs containing mercury, or old electrical appliances, each of which gives a very different set of environmental challenges. In an ideal world each should be dealt with separately.

G Before that can happen, though, we need to get a clearer picture of the life cycle of different kinds of waste, which is how the tracking project can give useful information. The team have designed tags that can be fixed to all kinds of rubbish, and these tags beam out their location every 15 minutes for up to two months. Each is built around a mobile phone SIM card and battery, and a motion sensor. A low-power microprocessor keeps track of the motion sensor and, when the sensor registers movement it switches on the

SIM card, triggering a search for nearby mobile phone towers. The SIM then sends an SMS containing this information to the team and the team's software compares it with the standard map of signal strength fingerprints to determine the position of the tag. The tags are not precise to the metre. In cities where there is a dense network of mobile phone towers, the team can locate an object to within 100 to 500 metres. In rural zones, that may be a kilometre or more.

H While tagging waste can identify where recyclables are being tossed into landfill, or where hazardous waste is illegally shipped overseas, there is a more fundamental reason to tag trash: to find out where society stores the materials that it mines from the Earth and temporarily turns into products. Today's landfill sites contain large amounts of important metals, including gold, zinc, aluminium, nickel, copper, cadmium and mercury – in many cases at higher concentrations than natural ore deposits – plus huge quantities of recyclable glass and plastic. As commodities become scarce in the following centuries, we may have to mine landfills for their riches, and that means finding out exactly where to start digging.

Questions 22–23

Choose TWO letters, A–E.

Write the correct letter in boxes 22 and 23 on your answer sheet.

According to the writer, which TWO of the following things need to happen?

A   Householders should be more aware of the waste-sorting process.

B   We need to find out how much waste is in the system.

C   We need to know more about the kinds of waste that have been thrown away.

D   Business and industry must follow established guidelines.

E   We should locate and reuse valuable resources.

Questions 24–27

Answer the questions below.

Choose NO MORE THAN THREE WORDS from the passage for each answer.

Write your answers in boxes 24–27 on your answer sheet.

24   Which item of rubbish does the writer use as an example to show the many ways rubbish can be dealt with?

25   Which city is involved in two stages of research?

26   What have people already tried hard to establish in order to get products to consumers?

27   What general term is used to cover a wide range of very different kinds of rubbish?

READING PASSAGE 3

You should spend about 20 minutes on questions 28–40.

Do animals think like humans?

A Some pet owners believe that their animals understand them when they speak, but how much do animals really understand of what we say? To what extent is their thinking a reflection of ours? Recent experiments have begun to throw light on the matter.

An Austrian dog – researchers call her Betsy – has a vocabulary of more than 300 words. 'Even our closest relatives, the great apes, can't do what Betsy can do – hear a word only once or twice and know that the acoustic pattern stands for something,' says cognitive psychologist Juliane Kaminski. 'Dogs' understanding of human forms of communication is something new that has evolved,' she says, 'something that's developed in them because of their long association with humans.' Scientists think that dogs were domesticated about 15,000 years ago, a relatively short time in which to develop language skills.

But how similar are these skills to those of humans? For abstract thinking, we employ symbols, letting one thing stand for another. Betsy, in an experiment, was shown a picture of a Frisbee, a picture she had never seen before, and told to find it. She brought the Frisbee from among other toys in another room.

B Other animals also have skills similar to those of humans. 'People were surprised to discover that chimpanzees make tools,' said Alex Kacelnik, a behavioural ecologist at Oxford University, referring to the straws and sticks chimpanzees use to pull termites out of their nests. 'But people also thought "Well, they share our ancestry – of course they're smart." Now we're finding these kinds of exceptional behavior in some species of birds. But we don't have a recently shared ancestry with birds. Their evolutionary history is very different; our last common ancestor with all birds was a reptile that lived over 300 million years ago. This means that evolution can invent similar forms of advanced intelligence more than once – that it's not something reserved only for primates or mammals.'

C Kacelnik and his colleagues are studying one of these smart species, the New Caledonian crow, which lives in the forests of the Pacific island of the same name. New Caledonian crows are among the most skilled of tool-making and tool-using birds, forming probes and hooks from sticks and leaf stems to poke into the palm trees where fat grubs hide. Since these birds, like chimpanzees, make and use tools, researchers can look for similarities in the evolutionary processes that shaped their brains. Something about the environment of both species favored the evolution of tool-making neural powers.

But is their use of tools rigid and limited, or can they be inventive? Do they have what researchers call mental flexibility? Chimpanzees certainly do. In the wild, a chimpanzee may use four sticks of different sizes to extract the honey from a bee's nest. And in captivity, they can figure out how to position several boxes so they can retrieve a banana hanging from a rope.

D Answering that question for New Caledonian crows – extremely shy birds – wasn't easy. Even after years of monitoring them in the wild, researchers couldn't determine if the birds' ability was innate, or if they learned to make and use their tools by watching one another. If it was a genetically inherited skill, could they, like the chimps, use their talent in different, creative ways?

To find out, Kacelnik and his students brought 23 crows of varying ages (all but one caught in the wild) to the aviary in his Oxford laboratory. Four hatchlings were raised in captivity, and all were carefully kept away from the adults, so they had no opportunity to be taught about tools. Yet soon after they fledged, all picked up sticks to probe busily into cracks and shaped different materials into tools.

E Birds can cheat too. Other studies by the same researcher show that western scrub jays can know another bird's intentions and act on that knowledge. A jay that has stolen food itself, for example, knows that if another jay watches it hide a nut, there's a chance the nut will be stolen. So the first jay will return to move the nut when the other jay is gone.

Such deceptive acts require a complicated form of thinking, since you must be able to attribute intentions to the other individual and predict that individual's behaviour.

F One school of thought argues that human intelligence evolved partly because of the pressure of living in a complex society of calculating beings. Chimpanzees, orang-utans, gorillas and bonobos share this capacity with us. In the wild, primatologists have seen apes hide food from the alpha male or steal his females. Kacelnik's study is the first to show the kind of ecological pressures, such as the need to hide food for winter use, that would lead to the evolution of such mental abilities. Most provocatively, his research demonstrates that some birds possess what is often another uniquely human skill: the ability to recall a specific past event.

Questions 28–32

Reading Passage 3 has six sections, **A–F**.

Which section contains the following information?

*Write the correct letter, **A–F**, in boxes 28–32 on your answer sheet.*

28 Animals cause difficulties for a dominant member of their group.

29 Young birds used skills without assistance from their parents.

30 Humans and two species of animal may descend from the same origin.

31 Animals' skills may come as a result of spending time with people.

32 Birds show dishonest conduct.

Questions 33–35

*Choose the correct letter, **A**, **B**, **C** or **D**.*

Write the correct letter in boxes 33–35 on your answer sheet.

33   The writer mentions the domestication of dogs in order to

    A   say how different they are from another species of animal.

    B   explain why they are easy to research.

    C   show how quickly they have learned.

    D   argue that they are suitable pets.

34   A western scrub jay has demonstrated

    A   an ability to trick other birds.

    B   a talent for copying other birds' calls.

    C   a skill at hiding sticks for digging grubs from trees.

    D   an aggressive way of behaving in the presence of other birds.

35   Kacelnik's research has shown that

    A   captive birds do not know how to to steal from other birds.

    B   birds can make use of their memories on later occasions.

    C   monkeys can remember what happened in the past.

    D   primates are affected by their social surroundings.

Questions 36–40

Do the following statements agree with the claims of the writer in Reading Passage 3?

In boxes 36–40 on your answer sheet write

YES	if the statement agrees with the claims of the writer
NO	if the statement contradicts the claims of the writer
NOT GIVEN	if there is no information on this

36   Scientists anticipated primate ability to employ implements.

37   Chimpanzees and New Caledonian crows had surroundings that prompted them to develop a skill.

38   Chimpanzees show that they enjoy the challenge of problem-solving.

39   Observation in the wild was able to show that crows learnt by copying.

40   Complex thought processes may be displayed by western scrub jays.

Reading Test 2

ALL ANSWERS MUST BE WRITTEN ON THE ANSWER SHEET.

The test is divided as follows:

Reading Passage 1 Questions 1 to 13

Reading Passage 2 Questions 14 to 27

Reading Passage 3 Questions 28 to 40

Start at the beginning of the test and work through it. You should answer all the questions. If you cannot do a particular question leave it and go on to the next one. You can return to it later.

TIME ALLOWED: 60 MINUTES

NUMBER OF QUESTIONS: 40

READING PASSAGE 1

You should spend about 20 minutes on questions 1–13.

Vines in the sky

A The farms of the future may be built right in the centre of your city. Suburban sprawl, combined with the vast economies of scale in operation in agriculture, have typically driven food production far from populated centres, with an increase in the cost of transport and risk of spoilage en route. However, the days of market gardens on the edges of urban areas supplying fresh food straight to your table may soon be over; mass city-centre farming may soon replace them. A visionary microbiologist and environmental lecturer, Dickson Despommier from Columbia University in New York, sees our future cities populated by a new kind of market garden. The creator of this radical 'vertical farming' idea describes the evolution of the concept from an older project involving rooftop gardening in Manhattan. While that was interesting, it couldn't be sustained on a mass scale. But it planted the seed of another idea. Looking at greenhouse projects in New York, the resulting concept was large-scale, indoor, urban agriculture in skyscrapers.

B Following this, Despommier set up laboratory projects aimed at different design challenges and attracted a wide range of enthusiastic collaborators and contributors. He believes this vertical farming method could be a solution to some of the world's most pressing issues. The world population is expected to grow by three billion to 8.6 billion over the next half century. By then, some 80 per cent of the world's population will live in cities, and they will need to eat. At the same time, conventional farm and grazing land takes up an enormous amount of space, with over one-third of the world's surface currently used for agriculture. Despommier figures that in the next five decades an area of new arable land roughly the size of Brazil will be required to feed the world's growing population – land that simply doesn't exist.

C Despommier's concept relies on using green methods of architecture and materials to build skyscrapers that house, grow and produce crops. New materials and technologies such as cheaper reflectors, which reflect sunlight where it's needed, more efficient solar panels for energy and system-wide recycling are integral to the plan. One unusual feature is the use of a type of shellfish to filter water. These can clean urban sewage to a state suitable for irrigation.

D 'Outside, one acre (0.4 of a hectare) of land means one crop a year,' says Despommier. 'Indoors, you can grow one crop every three months. You can get four crops a year.' He suggests that 150 such buildings could feed the entire city of New York for a year. Indoor crops require less pesticide and are less subject to the problems in nature, such as drought. Some academics say that a single skyscraper farm covering 1.3 hectares could produce enough food to feed 35,000 people for a year – the same as a 420-hectare farm. Each floor of the design would be rigged up with hydroponic watering systems and artificial lighting, and solar panels to provide electricity. However, vertical farming is not without its challenges. One is light – artificial lighting uses a great deal of electricity and generates considerable heat. Another is cost, with some A$93 million per building for construction and A$5.5 million a year for operation.

E   Among experts, opinions vary on whether the project can succeed. Creating conditions suitable for growth is a serious challenge, and some think the crop yield would be too low to make economic sense. 'My biggest reservation is that the basic premise is flawed. We already know how to increase food production from existing land resources, particularly in areas with surplus land such as sub-Saharan Africa. It's just that we do it incredibly badly at the moment,' says Rob Brook, a rural development researcher at the University of Wales in Bangor. 'This is a rich person's pipe dream.'

F   Yet there is strong support elsewhere. Luc Mougeout, an advocate of urban agriculture at Canada's International Development Research Centre, says the vertical farm is not only possible, but will happen within this generation. 'It would collect at one site a diversity of elements already at work in some form or another around the world,' he says. Despommier has the backing of his university as well as venture capitalists from the Middle East, China and the Netherlands.

If the vertical farming vision becomes a reality, we could find ourselves once again enjoying fresh fruit and vegetables sourced from just around the corner, except these might come from the 45th floor.

Questions 1–6

Reading Passage 1 has six sections, **A–F**.

Which section contains the following information?

*Write the correct letter, **A–F**, in boxes 1–6 on your answer sheet.*

NB You may use any letter more than once.

1   doubts about the feasibility of the project

2   the idea of moving market gardens from the outskirts to inner-city areas

3   how the system would avoid current agricultural problems

4   a previous program that was not practical for widespread use

5   sources of financial assistance to the proposal

6   a method of dealing with waste matter

Complete the notes below.

*Choose **NO MORE THAN THREE WORDS AND/OR A NUMBER** from the passage for each answer.*

Write your answers in boxes 7–10 on your answer sheet.

Despommier's solution to a world problem

Population within 50 years

▼   thought to reach **7** ....

▼   **8** .... living in urban areas

Land

▼   Proportion of Earth's area now used for farming: **9** ....

▼   Will need an extra area as large as **10** .... to provide food

---

Questions 11–13

Answer the questions below.

*Choose **NO MORE THAN THREE WORDS** from the passage for each answer.*

Write your answers in boxes 11–13 on your answer sheet.

11   How will the indoor farms get energy?

12   Besides the expense, what other challenge for indoor farms must be dealt with?

13   When does Luc Mougeout believe that Despommier's idea will become a reality?

READING PASSAGE 2

You should spend about 20 minutes on questions 14–27.

Movements of the planets

People have pondered the movements of stars and planets for as long as humans have been on this Earth. Long ago it was noticed that some of the lights in the sky seemed permanent in relation to each other and these were known as the 'fixed stars', whereas other lights moved about much more freely and were called 'the wanderers'. We now know the latter as the planets and we also know that the stars are by no means fixed but move in predictable patterns. That both stars and planets circled the sky over 24 hours was thought to be because they revolved around the Earth.

One early theory described the 'music of the spheres'. It was believed that the stars and planets were fixed on glass-like spheres that were centred on the Earth and created heavenly music as they moved, this latter belief possibly originating from the humming in the ears at high altitude. The Greek astronomer, mathematician and geographer Ptolemy was one of the first to suggest a pattern to these movements and in his Ptolemaic system the Sun, the Moon and the planets each had a sphere that moved independently of the others, and the stars were all fixed on the outermost sphere. This system was thus able to account for the differing movements then observed.

By the 16th century, more accurate measuring instruments were available, and using these, even before the telescope was developed, a Polish monk, Nicolaus Copernicus, spent much of his life making far more exact observations of the heavens. He tried to explain the mathematics behind the planets' movements but found that the circular movement of a sphere could not explain why, for example, Mars apparently stopped and went backwards for a short time. He discovered that the planets' movements could be far more easily predicted if not the Earth but the Sun were placed in the centre of the system, and the planets circled the Sun rather than the Earth. The problem with this explanation was that many people believed that man was the centre of the universe, and so not everyone accepted it. Copernicus avoided this difficulty by suggesting the theory merely as a method of more accurately working out the dates of important celebration days. The theory got strong support in the 17th century, when the eminent Italian mathematician and astronomer Galileo Galilei taught the Copernican system to his students.

The telescope was invented in the Netherlands in the early 17th century and this allowed far more accurate measurements of planetary motion to be taken. The German astronomer Johannes Kepler used it to discover that the Copernican observations were not quite correct and so could not be used to predict the orbits of the planets. Copernicus had assumed that the planets moved in a circular path around the Sun, but Kepler found that they did not; they moved in ellipses. He then developed his three laws of planetary motion, which gave a more exact method of estimating their orbits. The eccentric Danish astronomer Tycho Brahe had been appointed as the court astronomer to the Holy Roman Emperor and had made a large number of important observations that Kepler needed for his theories. However, although Kepler's three laws explained *how* the planets moved, they did not explain *why*. This was left to Isaac Newton in the 18th century.

Isaac Newton's invention of the reflecting telescope is often seen as a defining moment in the study of astronomy, but in fact he only enhanced it; the original telescope was invented in 1608 by the Dutchman Lippershey who used a convex lens in a tube focusing light into an eyepiece. The first telescopes

continued ▶

were seen as an important military invention to detect the distant approach of enemy soldiers before Galileo used one to observe the night sky. Newton discovered that a concave mirror reflecting light onto a flat secondary mirror gave an enhanced image, which allowed a much more accurate view of the heavens. Furthermore, mirrors were easier to manufacture than lenses and could be made larger, thus increasing the ability of astronomers to chart the movements of the stars and planets. Yet it was Newton's discovery of the laws of gravity that explained why the planets move the way they do. It also enabled two astronomers in the 20th century to predict the existence, before it was seen in telescopes, of another small, outer asteroid, Pluto (at first classified as a planet), by observing slight variations in the orbit of Uranus.

Questions 14–19

Look at the following statements (questions 14–19) and the list of people below.

Match each statement with the correct person, A–E.

Write the correct letter, A–E, in boxes 14–19 on your answer sheet.

NB You may use any letter more than once.

14 An alteration in the design led to an improvement in a scientific instrument.

15 The planets took an egg-shaped route.

16 The science at the time did not accord with what was observed in the sky.

17 The planets revolved around a different object than was previously thought.

18 A revolutionary theory provided reasons for the manner in which the planets travelled.

19 The use of a telescope provided evidence that amended what an earlier observer had found.

List of people

A Ptolemy

B Nicolaus Copernicus

C Galileo Galilei

D Johannes Kepler

E Isaac Newton

Questions 20–23

Complete the sentences below.

*Choose **NO MORE THAN THREE WORDS** from the passage for each answer.*

Write your answers in boxes 20–27 on your answer sheet.

20   Early observers used the term .... to refer to features that appeared

     to be motionless in the sky.

21   Objects that appeared to be mobile are now referred to as ....

22   According to an early way of thinking, ... was made by the motion

     of celestial bodies.

23   Ptolemy believed that each planet moved within its own ....

Questions 24–27

The diagrams show the basic differences between Lippershey's and Newton's designs for a telescope.

Label the diagrams below.

*Choose **NO MORE THAN THREE WORDS** from the passage for each answer.*

Write your answers in boxes 24–27 on your answer sheet.

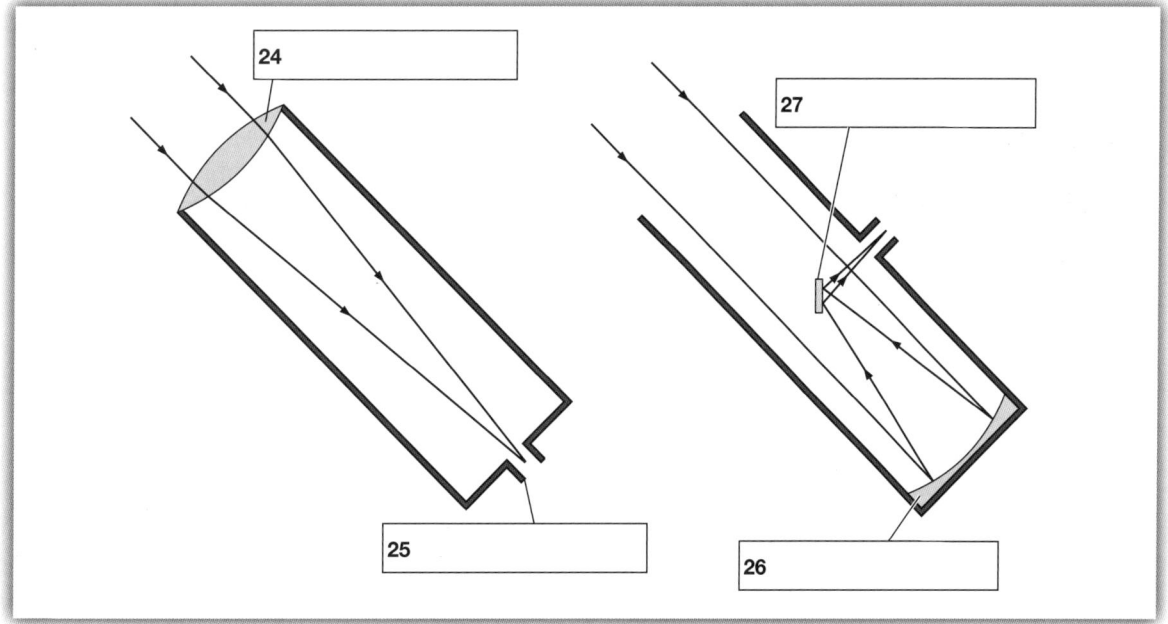

You should spend about 20 minutes on questions 28–40.

How and why does language change?

During the latter part of the 19th century, it was believed that a sound change affected the whole of a language at the same time: one sound system would smoothly develop into the next, and all words that contained a particular sound would be affected in the same way. We now know that such a change does not operate in a simple manner. Some speakers introduce the change into their speech before others; some use it more frequently and consistently than others and some words are affected before others. A more accurate view is to think of a change gradually spreading through the words of a language. At first just a few people use the change occasionally in common words; then a large number of words are affected, with the sound gradually being used more consistently; then the majority of the words take up the change.

The evidence for this kind of process has largely come from sociolinguistic studies of the variations in modern languages. These studies proceed on the assumption that variation in language use, which is found in any community, is evidence of the change in progress in a language. Detailed observations are made of the way in which different kinds of people speak in different social situations. The parameters that demonstrate these differences are known as *linguistic variables*. Examination of the frequency with which different people used a variable led to conclusions about the motivation, direction and rate of change in the language.

These are small-scale studies, but they have large-scale implications. It is likely that the same gradual process of change affects whole languages as well as dialects. The metaphor of a wave has proved particularly attractive since the late 19th century: a change spreads through a language in much the same way as a stone sends ripples across a pool. But even this implies too regular a movement to account for the reality of sociolinguistic variation.

It is easy to recognize a change in language – but only *after* it has taken place. It is not difficult to reflect on how people spoke several years ago to point to a new word that has recently entered the language. What is almost impossible is to *predict* a language change. Which sounds, words or grammatical construction will change in the next ten, twenty years?

It is just as difficult to be precise about the origins of a change in language. Who first used the new form? Where was it used? And when exactly? Historical dictionaries always give an approximate date of entry for a new word or meaning – but these dates invariably reflect the earliest known use of that word in the *written* language. The first use of the word in speech is always an unknown number of years previous to that.

To obtain answers to these questions, we need to know more about why language changes. If we understood the causes of change, we could begin to make predictions about when a change was likely to take place, and observe it while it was happening. There has long been imaginative speculation on the matter, with suggested causes coming from fields as far apart as theology and climatology (which is a consequence of human physical location – the mountain dweller having a physiologically different capacity for speech compared with the valley dweller). Some scholars have adopted a highly pessimistic view, feeling that the causes can never be found.

These days, the speculation and pessimism are being replaced by an increasing amount of scientific research, which has shown that there is no single reason for language change. Several factors turn out to be implicated, some to do with the nature of society, and some to do with the nature of language structure. When people move away from each other, their language will diverge. The two groups will have different experiences, and at the very least their vocabulary will change. Similarly, when people come into contact with each other, their language will converge. The sounds, grammar and vocabulary of one group are likely to exercise some influence on the other. These days, the increased mobility of people, within and between countries, makes this a major factor.

New objects and ideas are constantly being created, and language changes to accept them. At the same time, old objects and ideas fall out of daily use, and the language related to them becomes obsolete. Some change is the result of one population imperfectly learning the language of another. This is a common occurrence, as illustrated by many immigrant groups, or the levels of bilingualism found in contact areas. The minority language forms a small group that in the long term influences majority usage. For example, several varieties of American English display the influence of the West African linguistic background of its black population.

People come to talk like those they identify with or admire – a process that may be conscious or subconscious. Conscious change can be observed in those cases where people go out of their way to use or avoid certain features of their spoken or written language – such as happened with the English pronoun *whom*. Subconscious change, where people are not aware of the direction in which their speech is moving, is less noticeable, but far more common. The movement may be towards a favoured accent or dialect (one that has positive prestige), or away from one that is held in low esteem. The speakers are usually aware of the existence of linguistic differences (saying such things as *I don't like the way those people talk*), but unaware of any trend in their own speech related to their attitude.

Questions 28–34

*Choose the correct letter, **A**, **B**, **C** or **D**.*

Write the correct letter in boxes 28–34 on your answer sheet.

28   What do 'linguistic variables' do?

    A   They show how language is used differently by people.

    B   They prove that changes in languages are unpredictable.

    C   They record laws about how people should speak.

    D   They show which people introduce linguistic change.

29   What does the writer say is the relationship between changes in languages and in dialects?

    A   A minor change in a dialect will signal a major change in a language.

    B   Changes in languages are closely followed by changes in dialects.

    C   They begin rapidly then slow down.

    D   Neither of them happens suddenly.

30   When does the writer assert that a general language change can be recognised?

    A   when an item of vocabulary first comes into a language

    B   after a decade of usage in the language

    C   when the majority of people in a group have changed their way of speaking

    D   only following the occurrence of the change

31   According to the writer, why may location influence language change?

    A   Those from warmer places are more creative.

    B   Different environments may affect people's bodies.

    C   People living in hills need different expressions from those in valleys.

    D   Altitude affects the speed of language change.

32   What has recent scientific research illustrated?

    A   Influential people can dictate new language patterns.

    B   Difficult relationships between groups slow down change in language.

    C   Social aspects of language are the main influence on change.

    D   Language change has multiple causes.

33   How does increased mobility seem to affect language change?

    A   It speeds up the rate at which new languages are learnt.

    B   Those who travel can struggle to adopt the new language.

    C   People's language changes when they leave other members of their group.

    D   Dominant language traits are more easily transported.

34   Which aspect of language change is most often found?

    A   changes that the users themselves do not notice

    B   deliberate imitations to achieve status

    C   attempts by newcomers to improve pronunciation

    D   efforts to keep vocabulary up to date

Questions 35–40

Do the following statements agree with the claims of the writer in Reading Passage 3?

In boxes 35–40 on your answer sheet write

YES   if the statement agrees with the claims of the writer
NO   if the statement contradicts the claims of the writer
NOT GIVEN   if there is no information on this

35   Linguistic change occurs when a new pronunciation is adopted evenly.

36   Patterns in water are too even to be properly compared to patterns in language.

37   Historical dictionaries record the first spoken use of a new word.

38   In recent times, new vocabulary has primarily been introduced through the electronic media.

39   Change can happen when new speakers of a language make mistakes.

40   An established language can be influenced by an introduced language.

Reading Test 3

ALL ANSWERS MUST BE WRITTEN ON THE ANSWER SHEET.

The test is divided as follows:

Reading Passage 1	Questions 1 to 14
Reading Passage 2	Questions 15 to 28
Reading Passage 3	Questions 29 to 40

Start at the beginning of the test and work through it. You should answer all the questions. If you cannot do a particular question leave it and go on to the next one. You can return to it later.

TIME ALLOWED: 60 MINUTES

NUMBER OF QUESTIONS: 40

READING PASSAGE 1

You should spend about 20 minutes on questions 1–14.

The decline of Angkor Wat

A   Angkor is the scene of one of the greatest vanishing acts of all time. The ancient Khmer kingdom in modern Cambodia lasted from the 9th to the 15th century, and at its height dominated a wide area of South-East Asia, from today's Myanmar (Burma) in the west to Vietnam in the east. As many as 750,000 people lived in Angkor, its capital, making it the most extensive urban complex of the pre-industrial world. By the late 16th century, when Portuguese missionaries came across the lotus-shaped towers of Angkor Wat, the world's largest religious monument, the empire was in its final phase.

B   Exactly what caused the decline is not known; invaders, a change of religion, a shift to maritime trade that condemned an inland city are all guesswork. The people of Angkor left not a single word explaining their kingdom's collapse. Recent excavations, not of the temple itself but of the infrastructure that made the vast city possible, are suggesting a new answer. Angkor, it seems, was doomed by the very ingenuity that originally gave rise to it: the control of water, the most vital of resources, slipped away.

C   To ensure a steady water supply, stabilize rice production and control flooding, Khmer engineers had built a network of canals, moats, ponds and reservoirs. Massive earthworks slowed the wet-season deluge flowing from the Kulen Hills, directing it into canals that fed the barays (artificial bodies of water) and temple moats. Spreading across the gently sloping land, the water drained finally into the Tonle Sap, the largest freshwater lake in South-East Asia. This system guaranteed a water supply that did not rely on the monsoon. But this reliability required massive feats of engineering, including a reservoir called the West Baray, which is 8 kilometres long and almost three wide. To build this third and most sophisticated of Angkor's large reservoirs a thousand years ago, as many as 200,000 Khmer workers may have been needed to pile up nearly 16 million cubic yards of soil in embankments 300 feet wide and three stories tall. To this day the rectangular reservoir is fed by water diverted from the Siem Reap river.

D   Today's researchers have been amazed by the ambition of Angkor's early engineers. 'The entire landscape is artificial,' says one. Over several centuries, hundreds of miles of canals and dykes that relied on subtle differences in the land's natural inclination were constructed to divert water from three different rivers to the barays. During the summer monsoon months, overflow channels bled off excess water and, after the rains petered out in October or November, irrigation channels dispensed the stored water. The barays may have helped renew soil moisture by allowing water to soak into the earth. In surrounding fields, surface evaporation would have drawn up the groundwater to supply crops.

E   The clever water system may have made the difference between mediocrity and greatness. Much of the kingdom's rice was grown in fields with embankments that would otherwise have relied on monsoon rains or the seasonal flow and ebb of water on the floodplain. Irrigation

continued ▶

would have boosted harvests. The system could also have provided survival rations during a poor monsoon season, and the ability to divert and hold water would have afforded a measure of protection from floods. When other kingdoms in South-East Asia were struggling with too little or too much water, Angkor's waterworks would have been an extremely valuable asset.

F Curiously, there is good evidence that suggests the system was demolished by Angkor's own engineers; one of the huge spillways that was used to remove excess water had been destroyed. However, why this should have been done remains a complete mystery. The ruins of the spillway are a vital clue to an epic struggle that unfolded as generations of Khmer engineers coped with a water system that grew ever more complex and unruly. The most logical explanation is that a dam failed. The river may have chewed into the dam, gradually weakening it. Perhaps it was washed away by an unusually heavy flood, the kind that comes along every century or even every 500 years. The Khmer then ripped apart much of the stonework, salvaging the blocks for other purposes.

Questions 1–6

Reading Passage 1 has six paragraphs, **A–F**.

Which paragraph contains the following information?

*Write the correct letter, **A–F**, in boxes 1–6 on your answer sheet.*

1 a mention of increased food production

2 possible reasons for the destruction of an irrigation feature

3 a brief outline of a civilisation at its peak

4 an estimation of the labour force involved in the construction of the water system

5 modern-day reactions to a complex, man-made system

6 speculation about the fall of an empire

Questions 7–10

*Complete each sentence with the correct ending, **i–vi**, from the list below.*

*Write the correct letter, **i–vi**, in boxes 7–10 on your answer sheet.*

7   When visitors from the West arrived

8   When Angkor's irrigation worked well

9   When the third reservoir was constructed

10 When the monsoon failed

---

i   the water system was able to compensate.

ii   the stone blocks had disappeared.

iii   it outperformed neighbouring systems.

iv   a change was made that still exists today.

v   the system could use all the water supplied.

vi   the kingdom was in its last stages.

Questions 11–14

Do the following statements agree with the information given in Reading Passage 1?

In boxes 11–14 on your answer sheet write

TRUE   if the statement agrees with the information

FALSE   if the statement contradicts the information

NOT GIVEN   if there is no information on this

11 Missionaries accidentally damaged some structures at Angkor Wat.

12 Angkor's inhabitants left manuscripts providing information about the demise of their society.

13 The system at Angkor Wat took a few hundred years to construct.

14 Over the years, the irrigation system became harder to control.

READING PASSAGE 2

You should spend about 20 minutes on questions 15–28.

The need for bushfires

The plant communities that grow on the arid sandy soils of the south-western corner of Australia depend on fire for their survival. The land here is so poor in nutrients and in summer so baked by the sun that a forest of tall trees cannot grow. Instead there is a low bush mixed with a scatter of trees, few of which are more than 20 feet high. To botanists, however, it is a wonderland with flowers of great beauty, very few of which have been seen growing in the wild before. For this one corner of the continent contains no less than 12,000 different plant species and 87 per cent of them grow nowhere else in the world. This individuality stems from the fact that, 50 million years ago, Australia was partly covered by a shallow sea that separated the western part of the continent from the rest. As Australia gradually warmed, this sea dried up, but it left behind a wide expanse of sand, so that the western corner is cut off by desert and its ancient isolation is still to some extent evident.

Fire has regularly burnt this land throughout its recent geological history. The plants have evolved with it, so now they are not only well able to survive its destruction but have come to depend on it and use it to their own advantage.

The eucalypts or gum trees that grow there often take the peculiar form known as . Species that elsewhere become normal-looking trees grow here in such a different way that they might be thought to be a completely different kind. Instead of a single trunk that only has branches some height above the ground, they have a massive rootstock from which rise half a dozen thin trunks of a common height. To uninformed eyes it looks as if they had been trimmed to size. When fire sweeps through mallee, the slender trunks are often totally burnt and destroyed. But the rootstock, close to the ground or just below its surface, bears a ring of strong buds from which new stems rapidly sprout. They grow more quickly and vigorously than the old, partly because the ground has been recently fertilised by the ash of other plants, and partly because, to begin with, there are few survivors with such well-established root systems competing for those nutrients.

The bottlebrush, related to the eucalypts, produces spectacular clusters of bright red flowers at the end of its stems, which attract indigenous birds. But it will not shed any seed they produce unless there is a fire. So examining a bottlebrush can reveal how long it is since fire passed that way. All you have to do is to count the number of clusters of seeds still attached along the branch and that will tell you how many years the plant has remained unburnt.

The banksia, a tree belonging to the protea family, also relies on fire. It takes about a year for the seeds to mature. Like the bottlebrush, some banksias will not shed their seeds unless there is a fire. Indeed, it is almost impossible to remove them from the plant because they are held in hard, woody capsules. But as the flames burn the branches, the intense heat causes the capsules to open. By releasing their seeds only after a fire, the banksias ensure that they fall on well-cleaned, brightly lit ground recently fertilised with ash and so get the most favourable of starts in what is, even at best, an extremely harsh and demanding environment.

This country is also one of the headquarters of the grass tree, which is really neither a grass nor a tree. It is a distant relative of the lilies. But it does have very long narrow leaves that resemble grass, and they are borne in a great shock on the top of a stem that looks like the trunk of a tree and may be up to 10 feet high. However, the core of this trunk is not timber but fibre and what seems to be bark, is, in fact, the tightly compacted bases of the leaves, which are shed annually from beneath the crown as the plant grows higher. These bases are glued together by a copious flow of gum and they form a very efficient heat insulation. Since the plant sheds one ring of leaves annually, counting the rings of bases in this fireproof jacket gives an indication of age. When the bushfire flames do come, they quickly burn off the great tuft of leaves, which incinerate almost instantaneously. But the stem, surrounded by its fireguard, remains unharmed and the leaves are quickly regrown.

Questions 15–18

Complete the sentences below.

*Choose **NO MORE THAN THREE WORDS AND/OR A NUMBER** from the passage for each answer.*

Write your answers in boxes 15–18 on your answer sheet.

15 The south-western part of Australia is described as a .... for scientists

who study plants.

16 .... of the different kinds of plants in the south-western part of Australia

can only be found in that area.

17 .... once divided the Australian continent.

18 When the temperature in Australia slowly rose, the sea disappeared and a great area of

.... was left behind.

Questions 19–23

Choose the correct letter, A, B, C or D.

Write the correct letter in boxes 19–23 on your answer sheet.

19   What is unusual about the land in south-western Australia?

    A   It is cut off from the rest of the continent.

    B   The soil contains very little nourishment.

    C   It has many endangered plants.

    D   The soil composition has remained unchanged for many years.

20   What is the significance of fire to south-western Australia?

    A   It is an annual problem to the environment.

    B   It caused permanent damage to soil millions of years ago.

    C   Vegetation is reliant upon it.

    D   It keeps the area isolated from the rest of the continent.

21   What is mallee?

    A   a tree type that has multiple appendages rising from the ground

    B   a tree with a strong solid base above ground

    C   part of a tree that is beneath the surface

    D   the burnt remains of a desert tree

22   What effect does fire have on the bottlebrush tree?

    A   It will only grow in the ash left after a fire.

    B   The burnt plant appeals to birdlife.

    C   Fire prevents birds from destroying the plant.

    D   It will not release its seeds without a fire.

23   What effect does fire have on banksia growth?

    A   Fire carries seeds to more fertile areas.

    B   The ash from the fire destroys oxygen in the soil.

    C   The high temperatures force the seed cases to open.

    D   Fire destroys other plants that compete for resources.

Questions 24–28

Do the following statements agree with the information given in Reading Passage 2?

In boxes 24–28 on your answer sheet write

TRUE   if the statement agrees with the information
FALSE   if the statement contradicts the information
NOT GIVEN if there is no information on this

24   Most of the plants in their natural environment in south-western Australia are familiar to botanists.

25   Eucalypts in south-western Australia have a different appearance to eucalypts in other places.

26   Fire affects eucalypts in other parts of Australia as well as in the south-western region.

27   It is possible to tell the age of a bottlebrush by looking at it.

28   The composition of the grass tree is different from how it appears.

READING PASSAGE 3

You should spend about 20 minutes on questions 29–40.

Questions 29–35

Reading Passage 3 has seven paragraphs, **A–G**.

Choose the correct heading for each paragraph from the list of headings below.

*Write the correct number, **i–ix**, in boxes 29–35 on your answer sheet.*

List of headings

i	More attractive ideas for long-range space travel
ii	An ideal size of a possible source of power
iii	Stars too far to reach with present-day technology
iv	A plentiful supply of power in space?
v	Unlikely suggestions for interstellar travel
vi	The ageing process for space travellers
vii	Dangers of using dark matter as fuel
viii	A man-made power source
ix	Energy generated and speed reached using dark matter

29	Paragraph A
30	Paragraph B
31	Paragraph C
32	Paragraph D
33	Paragraph E
34	Paragraph F
35	Paragraph G

Reaching the stars

A   Our nearest star, Proxima Centauri, is 4.2 light years away – more than 200,000 times the distance from the Earth to the Sun. Such vast distances would seem to put the stars well beyond the reach of human explorers. Suppose we had been able to ride aboard NASA's *Voyager 1*, the fastest interstellar space probe yet built. *Voyager 1* is now heading out of the solar system at about 17 kilometres per second. At this rate it would take 74,000 years to reach Proxima Centauri.

B   What would it take for humans to reach the stars within a lifetime? For a start, we would need a spacecraft that can travel at close to the speed of light. There has been no shortage of proposals: vehicles propelled by repeated blasts from hydrogen bombs, or from the destruction of matter and antimatter. Others resemble huge sailing ships with giant reflective sails, pushed along by lasers. All of these ambitious schemes have their disadvantages, and it is doubtful they could really go the distance.

C   Now there are two radical new possibilities on the table that might just enable us, or at least our descendants, to reach the stars. One physicist has outlined his design for a spacecraft powered by dark matter, which is apparently extremely abundant, even if we cannot see it. And two mathematicians have proposed a craft powered by an artificial black hole.

D   Nobody disputes that building a ship powered by black holes or dark matter would be extremely difficult. Yet, remarkably, there seems to be nothing in our present understanding of physics to prevent us from making either of them. Most astronomers are convinced of the existence of dark matter because of the way its gravity pulls on the stars and galaxies we see with our telescopes. Such observations suggest that dark matter outweighs the universe's visible matter by a factor of about six. So a dark matter starship could pick up its fuel on the way and would therefore not need to carry any.

E   It is speculated that dark matter particles could be made to collide, thus annihilating each other and converting their mass to energy. One kilogram of dark matter could release 10 billion times more energy than 1 kilogram of dynamite. Even less certain is the detail of how a dark matter rocket might work. The matter could be collected and compressed, which would increase its annihilation rate, and the quicker it travels, the quicker it would scoop up its fuel and accelerate. It is thought that such a rocket might be able to come close to the speed of light within a few days.

F   Another possibility concerns the construction of a rocket using a black hole as fuel. Very small black holes emit far more radiation than large, stellar-mass black holes, according to the equations describing black holes. A black hole weighing about a million tonnes would make a perfect energy source, it has been calculated. It is small enough to generate enough radiation to power a starship, yet large enough to survive without radiating all its mass during a typical stellar journey of about 100 years in duration.

continued ▶

G Recently, one possibility is to hunt for a pre-existing black hole, but theorists have been sceptical and prefer an alternative proposal of making one. To create a black hole one would need to concentrate a tremendous amount of energy into a tiny volume of, say, 20 cubic metres. Solar energy would be collected in solar panels, each 250 kilometres across, orbiting just a few million kilometres away from the Sun and soaking up sunlight for about a year. The resulting million-tonne black hole would be about the size of an atomic nucleus. The next step would be to manoeuvre it into the focal range of a parabolic mirror attached to the back of the crew quarters of a starship. The resulting gamma ray photons would be the starship's exhaust and would push it forwards. A black-hole starship could accelerate to close to the speed of light in a few decades, it is thought, and once you were travelling at this speed in your starship, time would slow down for you, so you would age more slowly than your friends and family back on Earth.

Questions 36–37

*Choose **TWO** letters, A–E.*

Which **TWO** proposals to power superships might allow people to travel to the stars within a human lifespan?

Write the correct letter in boxes 36–37 on your answer sheet.

A   hydrogen bombs

B   laser-driven sails

C   black holes

D   dark matter

E   solar energy

Questions 38–40

Complete the summary below.

*Choose **NO MORE THAN ONE WORD** from the passage for each answer.*

Write your answers in boxes 38–40 on your answer sheet.

One theory proposes a collision of dark matter **38** ...., which would be mutually destroyed, thus resulting in a transformation of their physical components into

39 .... Such a procedure would be capable of producing vastly greater force than using a conventional explosive. Acquisition and compression of the matter would speed up its **40** ...., and the vehicle might approach light speed in a very short time.

Reading Test 4

ALL ANSWERS MUST BE WRITTEN ON THE ANSWER SHEET.

The test is divided as follows:

Reading Passage 1   Questions 1 to 14

Reading Passage 2   Questions 15 to 28

Reading Passage 3   Questions 29 to 40

Start at the beginning of the test and work through it. You should answer all the questions. If you cannot do a particular question leave it and go on to the next one. You can return to it later.

TIME ALLOWED: 60 MINUTES

NUMBER OF QUESTIONS: 40

READING PASSAGE 1

You should spend about 20 minutes on questions 1–14.

What are shares for?

A A company that is quoted on the stock exchange offers shares in its ownership to anyone who wants to buy them. A large company may issue millions of shares. There are several types of shares, but the most common are called 'ordinary' shares. If you buy one, you are a part-owner, or shareholder, in the company, with the right to share in its profits, to attend board meetings and to vote on key issues and appointments. You can sell your shares if someone is willing to buy them.

B The price of a share changes all the time: it may bear little relation to the cash value of the company if all its assets were to be sold. There have been many cases, for instance, where the buildings owned by a company were grossly undervalued and its share price was much lower than it should have been. On the other hand, when the stock markets of the world are booming, many companies are valued at much higher prices in the stock market than their 'real' value. And there are new challenges to valuation – how, for example, do you value a high-tech company whose products change every few months, and whose real earning power resides in the brains of its talented employees? The constantly changing difference between the market capitalization – which is essentially the total value of all a company's shares at the current market price – and the 'real' value is one of the great themes of stock market analysis.

C Shares are volatile – their prices go up and down all the time as people buy and sell them. All sorts of factors influence the prices of shares, including company analysis, political change, natural disasters, wars and economic fluctuations, but one of the main factors is the behaviour of people who buy shares, or, as some would have it, 'the madness of crowds'. If many investors think the price of a share is going to go up and buy it, the price of the share will go up until they stop buying. This may have nothing to do with the essential soundness of the company. This kind of volatility is temporary. In the long term, shares in good companies are thought to be better investments than those in bad ones. This might seem obvious, but in the intense world of the stock market, it is often forgotten.

D The capitalist system of financing big business is fundamental to the world's present economic system. Since the 1990s, there has been no other system that is a serious contender with it. Thus, like it or not, people who want to increase or preserve their assets must learn how it works, and will probably decide to participate in it at some time in their lives. The soundest, best-established companies are known as 'blue chips'. The term 'blue chip' comes from the world of the casino, where blue chips are those with the highest value. Next come the 'secondary issues', which are shares in solid companies. These receive slightly less confidence than the blue chips. 'Growth stocks' are shares in newer companies that are expected to do well in the future, but which may not do so. Finally, there are the 'penny shares', which are those of companies with a low value, but which may increase for some reason.

E Companies usually start out by being privately owned. When they get big enough, the owners may decide to 'go public' and sell part of the shares of their company on the stock market. The rules for going public are quite strict, to make sure that the company is worth buying. The advantage to the original owners of selling their shares is that, if the offering is successful, they can realize very large sums of cash. Some owners, however, prefer to keep control by staying private, while others have been known to buy back all the shares and return the company to private ownership. Taking a company listed on the stock market back into private ownership is quite rare, and when it is done the aim is usually to increase control over decision-making. For instance, tycoons may decide they can do a better job of building the business by making a company private because the red tape and potential for interference by other shareholders is much less.

Questions 1–5

Which paragraph contains the following information?

*Write the correct letter, **A–E**, in boxes 1–5 on your answer sheet.*

NB You may use any letter more than once.

1   a lack of connection between company viability and share price

2   the rights and responsibilities of those who own shares in a company

3   companies' reasons for seeking investment from shareholders

4   some reasons for changes in what people pay for shares

5   the basic pattern for business dealings worldwide

Questions 6–10

Answer the questions below.

*Choose **NO MORE THAN THREE WORDS** from the passage for each answer.*

Write your answers in boxes 6–10 on your answer sheet.

6   What kind of organisation may be difficult to place a value on?

7   What term is used for the combined value of shares in a company at a particular point in time?

8   Where does the expression used to describe the most secure shares come from?

9   What name is given to untested shares with recognised potential to rise in value but some risk?

10   Who, for example, might remove a company from the stock exchange, in order to have more control?

Questions 11–14

Do the following statements agree with the information given in Reading Passage 1?

In boxes 11–14 on your answer sheet write

TRUE   if the statement agrees with the information
FALSE   if the statement contradicts the information
NOT GIVEN   if there is no information on this

11   Shareholders have a say in who can hold important positions in the company.

12   A company can limit the number of shares held by any shareholder.

13   A significant factor in determining the cost of shares is buyer activity.

14   A company can easily decide to go public as there is little control of the process.

You should spend about 20 minutes on questions 15–28.

Australia's Royal Flying Doctor Service

Although Australia has roughly the same area as the United States, it supports a population that is less than 10 per cent of the total US population. The reason is that one-third of the country is mainly desert, another third is classified as arid and much of the rest contains soil with few nutrients. Consequently, the inland is very sparsely populated, and those who live and work there do not have access to the facilities that urban Australians have always taken for granted. The Royal Flying Doctor Service (RFDS) has over the past century provided medical services to those in the outback, as inland Australia is generally known. The service has made a huge contribution to the settlement of outback Australia, a blessing for scattered populations in times of medical emergency.

The first person to champion the need for an airborne medical serve in the outback was John Flynn (1880–1951). A church minister working in remote settlements, Flynn followed up on an idea first proposed in 1918 by a correspondent Lieutenant J. Clifford Peel of the Australian Flying Corps. Flynn took up the case for a service after helping to establish nursing homes in several outback towns. In his opinion, the patient should receive a doctor's visit rather than face the risk of further injury or illness by being forced to travel over inadequate roads to hospitals which could be several days' journey away.

Flynn's undertaking got the support of his church and government officials, and public donations began to come in. On 15 May 1928, the Australian Inland Mission Aerial Medical Service commenced business in Cloncurry, Queensland, and two days later the first flight took off. What was later to be called the Royal Flying Doctor Service was born. In its first year of operation, the service attended to 255 patients.

The effectiveness of the Flying Doctor is in its wide reach, and it wasn't long before it was expanding across the country. The goldfields of Western Australia had aircraft support for serious emergencies from 1931, although it was 1937 before the region officially had a Flying Doctor section. In 1935, Port Hedland got its service as did the Kimberley region with the help of Victorian philanthropists.

When the Flying Doctor started out, aviation equipment and facilities were still in their infancy. With no navigation aids on board or on the ground, pilots had to find their way using landmarks. Night flying was only considered in the most urgent of cases. Airstrips were rudimentary at best, and sufficient fuel had to be carried for the return trip. It was left to the pilot to decide if a landing could be made safely.

In its early days, the Flying doctor contracted aircraft owners and pilots to fly its medical staff where they were needed. The first contract was with Qantas, which leased out a four-passenger DH.50A along with equipment and staff at a rate of two shillings (A$0.40) per mile (1.6 km). That plane, named *Victory*, went on to fly 110 000 miles for the Flying Doctor until 1934. In 1949, the contract was transferred to Trans-Australia Airlines.

It was only in the 1960s that the RFDS had begun purchasing its own aircraft, and was employing pilots and engineers directly. While the early aircraft were predominantly

continued ▶

British, later models were American in design and manufacture. From single-piston engines to turbo props, from exposed cockpits to pressurised cabins also fitted out as flying intensive care units, the machines of the Flying Doctor have steadily advanced along with the aviation industry itself. The name, too, was to evolve over time. In 1942, the Australian Inland Mission Aerial Medical Service became the Flying Doctor Service, and in 1954 it was given a Royal Charter.

The RFDS now owns more than 50 modern aircraft operating from 21 bases throughout Australia flying the equivalent of 25 round trips to the moon each year. The flying doctors and nurses serve more than a quarter of a million people spread over the wide, open spaces of outback Australia. The RFDS is a non-profit organisation, its operations are funded by Commonwealth and State governments, public donations and corporate sponsorships.

The Flying Doctor has been a huge boon for the settlers of the outback. It has given endless comfort to far-flung populations who are that much safer in the knowledge that despite the distances involved, help in a medical emergency is not far away.

Questions 15–19

Do the following statements agree with the claims of the writer in Reading Passage 2?

In boxes 15–19 on your answer sheet write

YES	if the statement agrees with the claim of the writer
NO	if the statement contradicts the claim of the writer
NOT GIVEN	if there is no information on this

15 The Royal Flying Doctor Service caters for all Australians.

16 The first flying doctor was Lieutenant Peel.

17 The RFDS commenced in May 1928.

18 Longer flights were undertaken only at the discretion of the pilot.

19 The RFDS did not own any aircraft when it was founded.

Questions 20–25

Complete the summary using the list of words, A–I, below.

Write the correct letter, A–I, in boxes 20–25 on your answer sheet.

The RFDS in the sixties began **20** .... their own planes and were **21** .... crew

and maintenance staff. To begin with they bought aircraft from the UK, but later planes were

22 .... from the USA. In the first machines, pilots sat in the open air, but were later

23 .... with closed cabins, and full medical emergency facilities. These days, the RFDS

24 .... from 21 depots and **25** .... for over 250,000 patients annually.

A	equipped	**F**	caters
B	enlisting	**G**	acquired
C	flies	**H**	building
D	serves	**I**	hired
E	buying		

Questions 26–28

Complete each sentence with the correct ending, A–F, in the list below.

Write the correct letter, A–F, in boxes 26–28 on your answer sheet.

26 The RFDS has been successful mainly

27 Later aircraft were fitted out

28 Financial support for the RFDS comes

A with sophisticated facilities.

B largely from government taxes.

C due to its extensive spread.

D specially heated surgeries.

E from its competent staffing policy.

F from a variety of sources.

READING PASSAGE 3

You should spend about 20 minutes on Questions 29–40.

Questions 29–36

Reading Passage 3 has eight paragraphs, **A–H**.

Choose the correct heading for each paragraph from the list of headings below.

*Write the correct number, **i–xi**, in boxes 29–36 on your answer sheet.*

List of headings

i	Different ways that sound may have damaging effects
ii	Inability to detect depth of coastal waters
iii	The need to escape from predators
iv	Weather leads whales to food
v	Possible reason for double beaching
vi	The dangers of assisting a fellow whale
vii	Collecting the evidence for study
viii	An essentially Tasmanian problem
ix	A conclusive theory
x	A possible military involvement?
xi	Globules of air in the water

29   Paragraph A

30   Paragraph B

31   Paragraph C

32   Paragraph D

33   Paragraph E

34   Paragraph F

35   Paragraph G

36   Paragraph H

Why do whales beach themselves?

A A hundred corpses litter a beach in Tasmania, the smell of decaying whale flesh is everywhere. It's the first pod of whales to strand this season; perhaps the first of many. When the last stranded whale dies, as often happens, the story doesn't end there. A team of researchers, vets and other experts take body samples, collect skin, tissue and teeth samples, recording anything that could help them answer the crucial question: why did these whales strand themselves? There are plenty of theories, some more convincing than others. For years the reason why whales wash up on the beach has been a mystery. But bit by bit, whale corpses are giving up their secrets.

B When 70 small dolphins were stranded on the British coast in 2007, locals immediately blamed the armed forces. Fishermen had sensed unusual activity beneath the waves. In recent years, navy sonar has been accused of causing certain whales to strand. It's known that noise pollution from offshore industry, shipping and sonar can interfere with underwater communication – but can it really drive whales out of the ocean and onto our beaches?

C There are two theories about the effects of sonar. First, the noise can surprise the animal, causing it to swim too quickly to the surface, resulting in compression sickness (known to human divers as 'the bends'), which can block the blood supply to the brain and ultimately kill it. Second, soundwaves themselves can make bubbles with an effect very similar to that of compression sickness. But plausible as they may seem, these are still theories, and based on our comprehension of land-based animals rather than deep-diving whales. 'Furthermore,' points out one researcher, 'whales have been stranding for a very long time – pre-sonar. So it can't be just that.'

D When animals beach next to each other at the same time, the most common cause has nothing to do with humans at all. Some whale species, it appears, are just too friendly for their own good. If one of a group strands and sounds the alarm, others will try and swim to its aid, and will become stuck themselves. In a social group of animals it's not long before one animal's navigational mistake becomes dangerous and fatally affects the whole group.

E Data has revealed that all mass stranding sites around Australia were gently sloping sandy beaches, some with inclines of less than 0.5 degrees. For whales, shallow sandy beaches disrupt their echolocation system (the clicks that whales broadcast). On a gentle sandy beach the echo disappears so the whales assume there is no barrier ahead of them. When the whale doesn't hear any echo it continues to swim at full speed until it crashes onto the beach.

F But that's not all. Ralph James, a physicist, suggests that physics may be able to help with the 'when' as well as the 'where'. 'Rising bubbles,' he says, 'block some of the whales' echoes, and the ocean is full of bubbles. Larger ones quickly rise to the surface and disappear, while smaller ones – called microbubbles – can last for days. It's the smaller ones that absorb the whales' echolocation clicks. Rough weather generates more bubbles than usual and during and after a storm whales may essentially be swimming blind.' There seems to be some anecdotal evidence in favour of James' storm theory. Strandings in Tasmania often occur in quite wild weather. Rain droplets on the sea surface and large waves pounding the coast both add bubbles to water near the shore.

continued ▶

G Mass strandings have also been linked with sunspot cycles and some scientists believe that fluctuations in the Earth's magnetic field may be involved. Others are more sceptical about the sunspot connection. There is also evidence that the strandings are associated with major climatic cycles, years in which there are strong westerly and southerly winds that bring cool, nutrient-rich water closer to the southern Australian coast. This water contains plankton and fish, and the whales follow.

H Some wonder why many whales, once rescued from the beach, turn around and beach themselves once more. One possible explanation may lie in the harm the first beaching does. Sperm whales, for instance, due to their great size and weight, can die rapidly before rescuers can aid them; as they can weigh up to 30 tonnes and be up to 15 metres long, they are immediately in danger on the beach. While lying on the beach, they can topple over because their great weight is unsupported by water and fall onto a flipper. This prevents blood flow to the flipper, which is then rendered ineffective for its main purpose of steering. Consequently, when the whale is back at sea, it can no longer control its direction and often returns unintentionally to the beach to become stranded again.

Questions 37–40

Choose the correct answer A, B, C, or D.

Write the correct letter in boxes 37–40 on your answer sheet.

37 Why might an abnormal noise harm a whale?

    A   It can force the animal away from its companions.

    B   It can cause a startled whale to come up too fast.

    C   It can disturb communication between the animals.

    D   It can lead a whale to collide with a boat.

38 Why do some people discount the dangers of sonar to whales?

    A   It has not caused the death of whales for many years.

    B   The animals have got used to such sounds.

    C   Whales were beaching before sonar existed.

    D   Sonar usually only affects animals on land.

39 Why do whales fail to notice problems near shallow, sandy beaches?

    A   There is too much sand thrown up in rough water.

    B   The depth of the water decreases too suddenly for them to detect.

    C   Their focus is diverted by the prospect of food.

    D   The sloping beach suppresses the signals they need to navigate.

40 What evidence is cited to support James' theory about whale strandings?

    A   local weather patterns

    B   studies in magnetic fields

    C   injuries to whales

    D   observations of the sun

READING ANSWER SHEET

Pencil must be used to complete this sheet.

1			**21**		
2			**22**		
3			**23**		
4			**24**		
5			**25**		
6			**26**		
7			**27**		
8			**28**		
9			**29**		
10			**30**		
11			**31**		
12			**32**		
13			**33**		
14			**34**		
15			**35**		
16			**36**		
17			**37**		
18			**38**		
19			**39**		
20			**40**		
				Total	

Writing

What is in the writing module?

Format of questions	
Task 1	You have to describe information presented in a graph, table, chart or diagram by summarising and reporting the main features, trends or comparisons.
Task 2	You have to write a discursive essay on a given topic, presenting ideas that are relevant to the issue.
Time allowed	60 minutes It is suggested that you spend approximately 20 minutes on Task 1 and 40 minutes on Task 2. Your grade on Task 2 is worth twice as much as your grade on Task 1.
Number of words required	
Task 1	150 words minimum
Task 2	250 words minimum
Writing skills	See detailed guidelines in *Focusing on IELTS: Reading and Writing Skills* (Lindeck, Greenwood and O'Sullivan 2011). Task 1: pages 143–69 Task 2: pages 170–206

Tips for doing the Writing Test

Timing

▼ You have a total of 60 minutes – watch the time carefully.

▼ Allocate about 20 minutes for Task 1 and 40 minutes for Task 2.

▼ You can do Task 1 or Task 2 first.

▼ Task 2 is worth more marks than Task 1.

▼ Just before the hour is up, spend a few minutes checking your writing.

▼ If you find a mistake, cross out the error and write the correct version above it.

▼ Your writing needs to be clear so that it is easy for the examiner to understand what you have written.

▼ When preparing for the test, do the writing tasks under test conditions: write by hand, keep to the time limit and do not use dictionaries.

Make a plan

▼ Make a brief plan before you start writing.

▼ You can write your plan on the question sheet.

▼ A couple of minutes spent on a plan will help you produce a more logically structured answer that deals with all parts of the question.

Answer the question

▼ Pay careful attention to the question.

▼ Write an answer that is relevant to the task.

▼ Read the question several times while writing your answer to remind yourself what it is about.

▼ Make sure that you keep to the point.

▼ Answer each part of the question.

Paragraphs

▼ Task 1 should usually contain at least three paragraphs.

▼ Task 2 should usually contain at least five paragraphs.

▼ Make the beginning of a new paragraph clear by indenting or by leaving a blank line between paragraphs.

▼ Each paragraph covers a separate point.

▼ Use whole sentences – notes or bullet points are not acceptable.

Length

▼ If you do not write at least the minimum number of words for each task, you will be penalised.

▼ Do not waste time during the test counting the number of words you have written.

▼ While practising, you can get an idea of approximately how long an essay of 150 or 250 words is.

▼ Do not copy the question in your answer – a copied question is not included in the overall word count.

▼ You do not get a better score for writing an answer that is much longer than the minimum requirement.

Task 1

▼ You have to describe the information contained in a graph, table, chart or diagram.

▼ You may be required to describe the stages in a process or how something works.

▼ There may be more than one graph, table, chart or diagram.

▼ You have to summarise and report the main features and trends.

▼ Write about connections, comparisons and contrasts.

▼ Look carefully to see whether it is about percentages, millions or thousands.

▼ Determine whether it refers to the past, present or future, or to all three.

▼ Do not speculate on the reasons for the statistics.

▼ Provide data – do not just describe trends.

▼ The style should be formal.

Task 2

▼ Task 2 essays are longer and may require more thought and planning.

▼ You may have to argue for and/or against something, give your own opinion, describe a situation in your country or say what you think should be done.

▼ Your introductory paragraph should usually outline your answer to the specific question.

▼ Your main body paragraphs should expand on these thoughts, covering one main idea in each paragraph.

▼ You should develop the ideas and give some details and/or examples.

▼ Make sure that your answer is relevant to the actual question that has been asked – if the question contains the word 'environment', for example, do not simply start writing about pollution or climate change.

▼ Read the question several times while writing your answer to remind yourself what it is about and to avoid going off on a tangent.

- ▼ Try to vary the length of your sentences.
- ▼ Do not experiment with very long sentences if you are not sure of your grammar.
- ▼ Your final paragraph can be quite short and may summarise your answer, but do not simply repeat the words of your opening paragraph.
- ▼ The style should be formal.

Assessment criteria

In each task you are assessed using the following four criteria: answering the question, coherence and cohesion, vocabulary, and grammar.

Answering the question

The examiner will assess to what extent you have answered all parts of the question in the correct format and how much detail you have provided.

In Task 1 you need to provide an overview of trends, differences or stages, describe the main features and include some data.

In Task 2 you need to answer all parts of the question using the appropriate format of an essay with relevant, detailed ideas and arguments. There should be an introductory as well as a concluding paragraph.

Coherence and cohesion

Your answer needs to flow so that it is a structured piece of writing rather than just a number of unconnected sentences. This requires you to use sequencers, referencing, substitution and linking devices, and you need to arrange the information logically.

In Task 1, using paragraphs to focus on each important feature will help you to write a coherent response.

In Task 2, effective paragraphing is essential to organise a coherent argument, with one main idea in each paragraph.

Vocabulary

You should try to use a range of vocabulary that is appropriate to the type of writing, and to demonstrate a capacity to paraphrase. Correct spelling is important. You can use either British English or American English spelling, but it should be consistent. It is not a good idea to use a lot of very long and unusual words, as it is easy to use them wrongly.

Grammar

Your writing is assessed on the variety of grammatical structures used and how accurate they are. You can get a higher score if you use complex structures with subordinate clauses rather than only short, simple sentences. Punctuation is assessed as part of grammar.

Writing Test 1

Writing Task 1

You should spend about 20 minutes on this task.

The bar chart below shows the most important causes of stress for different age groups in Canada.

Summarise the information by selecting and reporting the main features, and make comparisons where relevant.

Write at least 150 words.

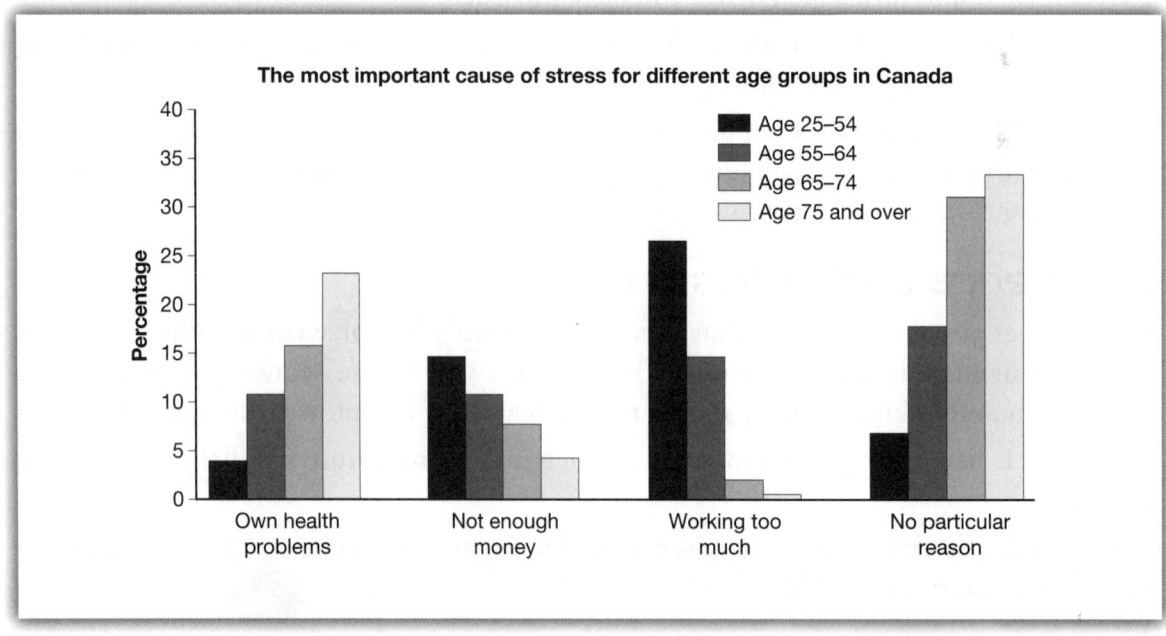

Writing Task 2

You should spend about 40 minutes on this task.

Write about the following topic:

> *Mobile phones and the Internet have made it easier to stay in contact with other people. However, as a lot of time is spent using telephones and computers, there is less face-to-face contact and direct communication.*
>
> *Is the growing use of communications technology a positive or a negative development for society?*

Give reasons for your answer and include any relevant examples from your own knowledge or experience.

Write at least 250 words.

After you have completed this practice test, check pages 164–5 of the answer key for sample answers.

Writing Test 2

Writing Task 1

You should spend about 20 minutes on this task.

The graphs below show the numbers and the percentages of children (aged 0–14) and young people (aged 15–24) in the Australian population from 1958 to the present, and projections until 2038.

Summarise the information by selecting and reporting the main features, and make comparisons where relevant.

Write at least 150 words.

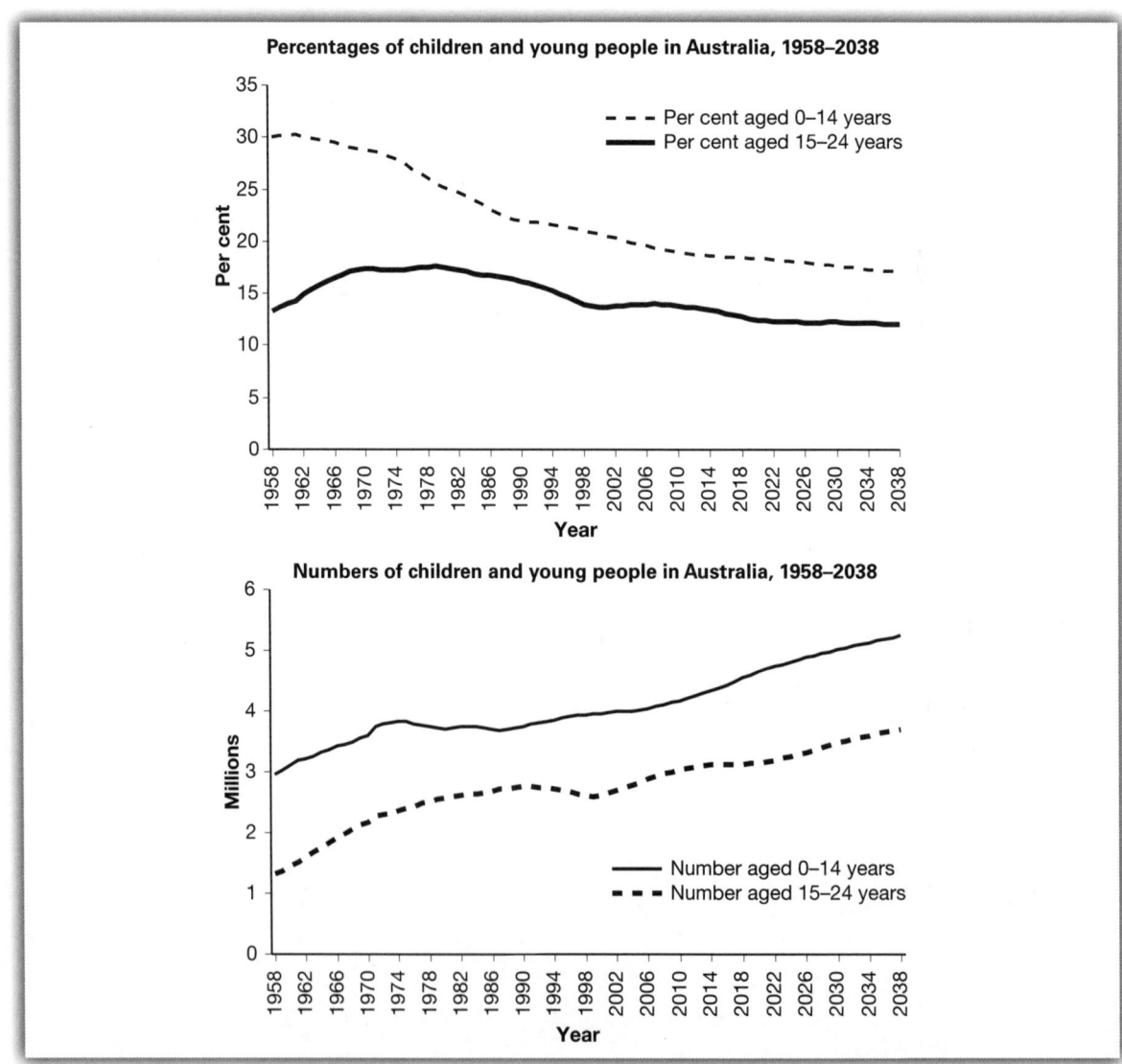

Writing Task 2

You should spend about 40 minutes on this task.

Write about the following topic:

> *In some large cities, people have to pay a fee when they drive their cars into the city centre, in a policy to reduce the number of cars in the city.*
>
> *Give reasons in support of and opposing this policy, and give your own opinion.*

Give reasons for your answer and include any relevant examples from your own knowledge or experience.

Write at least 250 words.

After you have completed this practice test, check pages 165–6 of the answer key for sample answers.

Writing Test 3

Writing Task 1 ✓

You should spend about 20 minutes on this task.

The diagram below shows how electricity is generated by using hot water from underground.

Summarise the information in the diagram to explain how the system works.

Write at least 150 words.

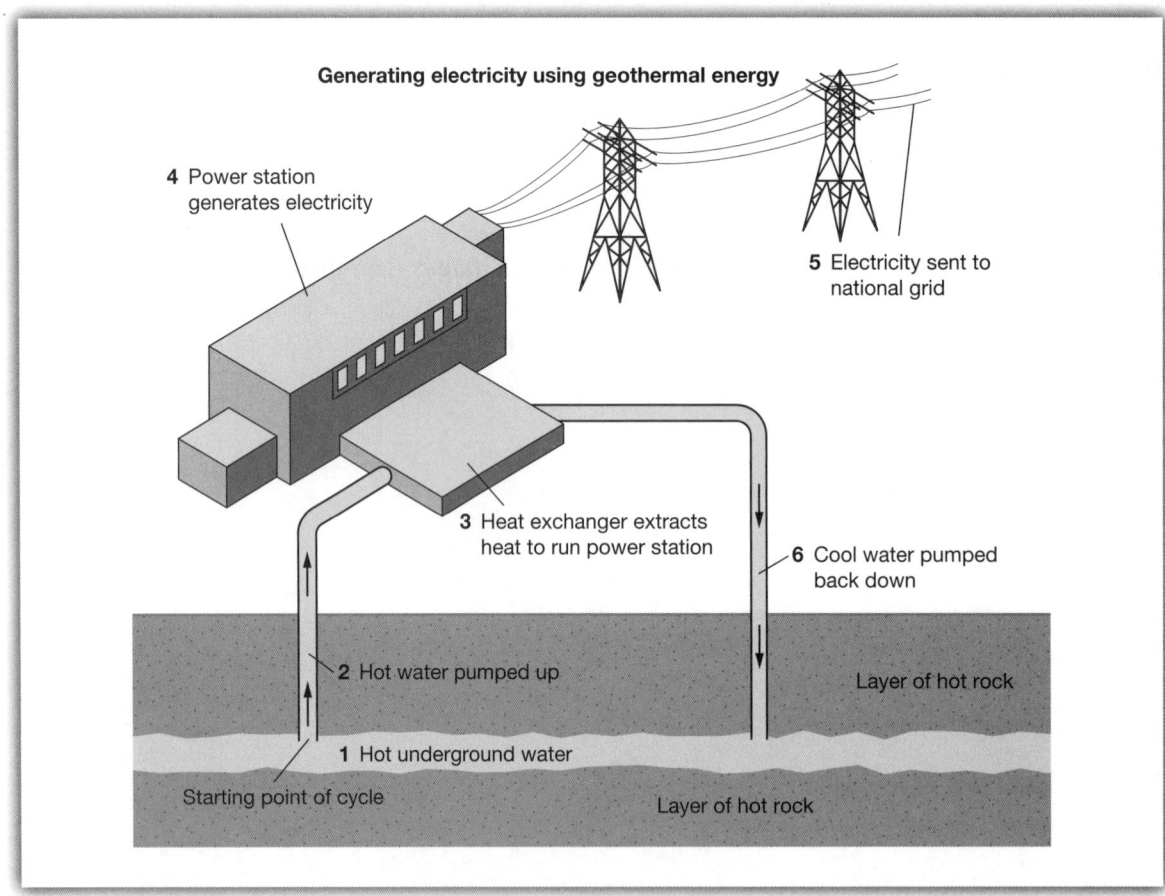

Generating electricity using geothermal energy

4 Power station generates electricity

5 Electricity sent to national grid

3 Heat exchanger extracts heat to run power station

6 Cool water pumped back down

2 Hot water pumped up

Layer of hot rock

1 Hot underground water

Starting point of cycle

Layer of hot rock

Writing Task 2

You should spend about 40 minutes on this task.

Write about the following topic:

> *In some countries, many people do not have enough money to access the Internet.*
> *Should governments be responsible for ensuring that everyone can get access to*
> *the Internet?*

Give reasons for your answer and include any relevant examples from your own knowledge
or experience.

Write at least 250 words.

After you have completed this practice test, check pages 166–7 of the answer key for
sample answers.

Writing Test 4

Writing Task 1

You should spend about 20 minutes on this task.

The table below shows the rate at which people saved money, expressed as a percentage of GDP, in seven countries from 1990 to 2008.

Summarise the information by selecting and reporting the main features, and make comparisons where relevant.

Write at least 150 words.

Country	Savings as a percentage of GDP*		
	1990	2000	2008
China	35.6	37.3	53.2
Germany	25.3	20.2	26.0
India	23.0	23.8	33.6
Italy	20.8	20.6	18.2
Singapore	43.6	46.9	48.3
South Korea	37.7	33.6	31.9
United States	15.3	17.7	12.1

* GDP (gross domestic product) is the total value of all goods and services produced in a country in one year.

Writing Task 2

You should spend about 40 minutes on this task.

Write about the following topic:

> *Some countries have laws that prohibit animals being used in circuses or other forms of entertainment because it is cruel to keep animals in an environment that can cause them stress.*
>
> *Should all countries have laws to prevent animals being used in circuses and similar forms of entertainment?*

Give reasons for your answer and include any relevant examples from your own knowledge or experience.

Write at least 250 words.

After you have completed this practice test, check pages 167–8 of the answer key for sample answers.

Speaking

What is in the speaking module?

This test is the same for Academic and General Training candidates.

Time allowed	11 to 14 minutes
Procedure	The Speaking Test is normally the last part of the IELTS test. It is conducted as a face-to-face interview and is recorded.
The format	There are three parts to the test. Each part has a different format. **Part 1:** Introduction and interview (4 to 5 minutes) First the examiner greets you and checks your ID. Then the examiner asks you questions about yourself, for example, about where you live, your work, study, interests and other familiar topics. These topics may include matters such as food, travel and entertainment. **Part 2:** Individual long turn (3 to 4 minutes) You have to talk about a topic connected to your own experience. The examiner hands you a card with the topic on it and gives you some paper and a pencil to make notes. You have one minute to read the card and think about what you're going to say, then the examiner asks you to talk for one to two minutes. The examiner tells you when to stop. After you have finished, the examiner might ask you one or two follow-up questions. **Part 3:** Discussion (4 to 5 minutes) The examiner engages you in a discussion about topics that have the same general theme as Part 2, but the questions are of a general rather than a personal nature. Some questions are concrete, others are more abstract. For detailed explanation see *Focusing on IELTS: Listening and Speaking Skills* (Thurlow and O'Sullivan 2011) pages 65–76.
Speaking strategies and skills	See detailed guidelines in 'Speaking strategies and skills', *Focusing on IELTS: Listening and Speaking Skills* (Thurlow and O'Sullivan 2011), pages 77–126.

Tips for doing the Speaking Test

In the Speaking Test the examiner has to follow a standard structure and ask a series of questions. It is an opportunity for you to show how good your spoken English is, so it's better to give detailed answers rather than very short answers. It's normal to feel nervous during the interview, so you don't need to tell the examiner that you're nervous or that you need a good score. The topics used in all parts of the Speaking Test are chosen so that the average person can talk about them without much difficulty.

Part 1

▼ Listen carefully to the questions and try to give relevant answers.

▼ If you don't understand a question, you can ask the examiner to repeat it.

▼ If there's a word you don't understand, you can ask the examiner to explain it.

Part 2

▼ Listen as the examiner reads out your topic.

▼ If you don't like the topic that you are given or you don't know much about it, you still have to talk about it.

▼ Read the candidate's card carefully.

▼ Determine whether you are being asked to talk about something that happened in the past, or about a situation now or something that may happen in the future.

▼ Use the minute to prepare by making a few notes about what you are going to say.

▼ Use the appropriate tenses for the context.

▼ While you talk, you can look at your own notes and the candidate's card to remind yourself of what you wanted to say.

▼ Don't worry about the time – the examiner will stop you after the two minutes are up.

Part 3

▼ After the monologue of the individual long turn in Part 2, the examiner will ask you a series of questions.

▼ If you don't understand a question, you can ask the examiner to clarify it.

▼ Your English is being assessed, not your knowledge.

▼ If you say things that are not true or not factually correct, you will not be penalised.

Assessment criteria

You are assessed on four criteria: fluency and coherence, vocabulary, grammar and pronunciation.

Fluency and coherence

▼ Try to keep speaking without a lot of hesitation or repetition.

▼ Connect sentences and ideas so that there is a smooth flow to what you say and it makes sense.

Vocabulary

▼ Use vocabulary accurately, flexibly and appropriately.

▼ Use paraphrase and idiomatic language.

▼ You are not expected to speak in a formal style or to use academic vocabulary.

▼ You can gain a higher score if you go beyond basic vocabulary and can use some less common words and expressions correctly.

Grammar

▼ Use a variety of grammatical structures accurately.

▼ You can get a higher score by using complex sentences with subordinate clauses rather than only short, simple sentences.

Pronunciation

▼ Speak clearly and use features of spoken language (stress, intonation and rhythm) to communicate effectively.

▼ This includes pronunciation at the level of individual words and of sentences.

▼ If you speak very quickly, it may be difficult to understand you at times, which will affect your mark.

▼ If you speak very slowly or hesitate a lot, there will not be sufficient connected speech for the features of good pronunciation to appear.

Sample speaking tests

In this section full transcripts are provided for the three complete recorded **sample speaking tests** on the CD that accompanies this book. The topics and questions used in these recorded sample tests are given first, so you can also practise giving your own answers to these questions and compare your answers to those given by the recorded candidates. An analysis of the performance of each of the three candidates can be found in the answer key at the back of the book.

The recorded sample speaking tests are followed by six complete **practice speaking tests**. The questions only for these tests are on the CD. For these practice tests, you should listen and pause after each question so you can practise answering it. If you work with a study partner, your study partner can read the questions for you to answer. You may find it useful to record your own answers and then listen to and analyse your own performance.

Remember that in the IELTS test, the examiner will sometimes ask you 'follow-up' questions after you have responded – questions such as 'Why?' or 'Why not?' or 'Can you tell me a bit more about that?' You can hear this in the recorded sample speaking tests and see it in the transcripts. When you answer the questions in the practice speaking tests, try to give more information, as if an examiner had asked you a follow-up question.

Sample speaking test

When you listen to the recording, after you hear each question you should press 'pause' and answer the question before going on to the next question.

Part 1 Introduction and interview

Hello. Could you say your full name, please?

And can I see your passport?

Thank you. Now, in the first part of the test, I'd like to ask you some questions about yourself.

Let's talk about what you do.

Why did you decide to study English?

Is it an interesting subject to study?

Do you have plans to do further study?

Now let's go on to the topic of reading magazines.

What kinds of magazines are popular in your country?

Why do some people prefer to read magazines rather than books?

Can you learn anything from magazines?

Now I'd like to talk to you about drinks.

What are some of the most popular drinks in your country?

Are there any drinks that people have at special times?

Are there any hot drinks that you like?

What do you think are the healthiest drinks?

Part 2 Individual long turn

Now we have the second part of the Speaking Test. I'm going to give you a card about a topic and I'd like you to talk about it for one to two minutes. Before you start, you can have one minute to think about what you are going to say. If you want to, you can make some notes. Do you understand? Here's some paper and a pencil for making notes and here's your topic.

I'd like you to describe a house or an apartment that you have lived in and which you liked.

Describe a house or an apartment you have lived in and which you liked.

You should say:

    when you lived there

    how it looked inside

    what kind of area it was in

and explain why you liked living there.

All right? Remember you can talk for one to two minutes. I'll tell you when the time is up. Could you start speaking now, please?

All right, thank you.

Part 3 Discussion

All right, thank you. You've been talking about a house or an apartment you have lived in, and now I want to discuss a few more general questions connected to this. Firstly, let's look at finding a place to live.

How do people usually find a place to live in your country?

What factors do you think determine where people choose to live?

What is it like to live in an apartment compared to living in a house?

Let's now look at home ownership.

Do most people rent their homes or own their homes where you're from?

Could you compare the attitudes of someone who's renting a home and someone who owns their own home?

Should the government help people buy their own homes?

Let's now look at residential areas.

Why do you think some residential areas are more pleasant to live in than others?

Could you compare living in the centre of the city and in a suburban area?

What are the benefits of planning a residential area before people start living there?

Thank you very much. That is the end of the Speaking Test.

SPEAKING

CD 3 · Track 2

Sample speaking test: Candidate 1

Examiner: Good afternoon. Can I have your full name, please?

Candidate: Hasan Can Yuksel.

Examiner: All right, and can I see your passport, please?

Candidate: Yeah, sure.

Examiner: Thank you. That's fine. Uh, now, in the first part of the test, I'd like to ask you some questions about yourself. Um, let's talk about what you do. Are you a student, or do you have a job?

Candidate: Yeah, I am a student. I'm a student in English class.

Examiner: And why did you decide to study English?

Candidate: Er, before, because I want to study in Masters, at Masters program, er, that's why I have to study English and I have to get a IELTS score. That's why I study English.

Examiner: OK. Is it an interesting subject to study?

Candidate: Yeah. It's, er, IT, my study, er ...

Examiner: Your Masters?

Candidate: Yeah, my Masters, yeah.

Examiner: Oh, OK. And why did you decide to study IT?

Candidate: Er, because I like technology and, er, you know IT is, er, related about information and management people. That's why.

Examiner: OK. Um, now let's go on to the topic of reading magazines. Um, what kinds of magazines are popular in your country?

Candidate: Er, gossip, er, magazines popular in my country actually and, er, and also those post magazine.

Examiner: OK. So why do some people prefer to read magazines rather than books?

Candidate: Because magazines, er, has a hot topic and eh, eh, er, that's the people interested in this gossip or sports program. That's why the people prefer to magazines.

Examiner: OK. And can you learn from magazines?

Candidate: Uh, sorry?

Examiner: Can you learn from magazines?

Candidate: No, I ... I prefer to newspaper to read.

Examiner: Why's that? Why is that? Why do you prefer to read newspapers?

Candidate: Er, because, er, my first degree is economy. I have to, er, learn to economy news and that's why and I don't interest gossip and sport activities.

Examiner: So, do you often read magazines?

Candidate: No.

Examiner: OK.

Candidate: No I don't read often.

Examiner: OK. Um, now I'd like to talk to you, um, about drinks.

Candidate: Yeah.

Examiner: What are some of the most popular drinks in your country?

Candidate: In my country is mopular, eh, most popular drinks is special Turkish drinks is alcohol, eh, it's, er, we call draku. It's, er, has, er, high level of alcohol inside.

Examiner: Uh-huh, OK.

Candidate: And beer, also.

Examiner: Right. Are there any drinks that people have at special times?

Candidate: Um, yes, birthdays or some celebrates, er, New Year celebrates, people prefer to drink.

Examiner: Mm. Right. OK. Um, are there any hot drinks that you like?

Candidate: Yeah, we, er, drink a tea but hot. Er, we prefer to hot tea, not iced tea and coffee as well.

Examiner: Mm. OK. And, um, what do you think are the healthiest drinks? What do you think are the healthiest drinks?

Candidate: Er, I like healthiest drinks, especially milk, um, yeah, er, yeah, just milk I think.

Examiner: OK. All right. Well, now we have the second part of the Speaking Test. I'm going to give you a card about a topic, and I'd like you to talk about it for one to two minutes. Before you start, you can have one minute to think about what you are going to say, and if you want to, you can make some notes.

Candidate: Mm hm.

Examiner: Do you understand?

Candidate: Yeah, I understand.

Examiner: All right. So here's some paper and a pencil for making notes, and here's your topic.

Candidate: Thank you.

Examiner: I'd like you to describe a house or an apartment you have lived in and which you liked.

You can see the candidate's card for this speaking test on page 100.

Candidate: Er, I wanna …

Examiner: All right, so remember, you can talk for one to two minutes, and I'll tell you when the time is up. Right? Can you start speaking now, please?

Candidate: OK. I will describe my, er, apartments in my country. Eh, it's, ah, ooh, my apartments has a, er, eight level, eight floor, and we lived in, er, seventh floor, and I like, I like it because this apartments has, er, a lot of, er, er, some, er, we have a swimming pool and tennis courts, er, it has a lots of facility, er, for, er, social life and, er, I used to, er, I used to both of them. And, um, we, er, our apartments is, er, in Istanbul in Turkey, and, er, it's, er, it has a, er, our home flat, er, has, er, three rooms and, er, has a huge, really huge kitchen and my mum actually, er, like it, like the huge kitchen and, um, it's, er, very close to our shop and we can go by walking. It's, er, and, er, this is, er, this house, this apartments, er, a little, er, suburb, little far to centre in Istanbul, but I like it, it's not crowded. Our area's so quiet and the people is, er, elite people and, er, our neighbours also is, er, kind peoples and we talking to neighbours, er, always and, er, we visit each other forgot my neigh ... our neighbours and, er, we have a good relation in our apartments.

Examiner: So, is your home similar to most other places in the area?

Candidate: Er, little different, not similar, little different, a little, er, high quality than the others.

Examiner: And has that area changed since you first lived there?

Candidate: Yeah, it's changed because, er, this, er, building, this apartments, er, built, er, several years ago, maybe, er, seven years ago, and after the finished this apartments, it's changed, this area is changed.

Examiner: All right, thank you. You've been talking, um, about a house or an apartment you have lived in, and now I want to discuss a few more general questions connected to this. Um, firstly, let's look at finding a place to live. Um, how do people usually find a place to live in your country?

Candidate: Er, the people, er, find a quiet place to live in my country because the centre is so crowded and so noisy. The people prefer to quiet place.

Examiner: And what other factors do you think determine where people choose to live?

Candidate: Others, er, I think main factor is, er, their jobs, the people's jobs because it's, er, really big problem in the, er, metropol cities, er, the traffic you know, lots of cars and crowded. You must go early every time and this is other factor for choose their apartments.

Examiner: Right. All right, and can you compare for me, say, in Istanbul, um, living, what it's like to live in an apartment compared to living in a house?

Candidate: Ah yeah. Er, my apartment has, I like my apartments, but, er, I, er, wants to live, er, er, good view, has a good view apartments and maybe he, er, I ... when I look at the window I can see a ocean or river or like this or lake.

Examiner: But, generally, what are the differences between living in an apartment and living in a house, say, in a city like Istanbul?

Candidate: Ah, it's too different, it's too different. Er, in Istanbul the people generally live in the apartment, but if you live in the houses, er, you have, er, not good relationships for their neighbours. Because it's different in Turkey. Er, if you live apartment you can get easily, er, a friend and yeah it's advantage for make a good relationships.

Examiner: OK. Um, let's now look at, um, home ownership. Um, do most people rent their homes or own their homes where you're from?

Candidate: In Turkey, eh, most people, eh, buy a home, not rent because this, er, our home prices is not, er, high. Is quite cheap, and you can get easily a home.

Examiner: OK.

Candidate: Because the people prefer to buy, buying a home.

Examiner: Right. So, what do you think the difference would be? What are the different attitudes between someone who's renting a home and someone who owns their own home? What's their attitude towards that home? Do you think there's a difference between a renter and an owner?

Candidate: Yes, er, there are lots of advantage or disadvantage, er, the rent or owner and if you rent a house, you can, eh, you must, er, moving, eh, you can be moved other places and always you must be ready to move, yes. But if you own the house, the, er, one disadvantages own the house, you can, you live, always you live the same place and you never change in your tirement, and all the same, all the people the same.

Examiner: Right.

Candidate: But if you're a renter you can change and you can get new friends, you can see a new place.

Examiner: Right. Right, well let's now look at, um, residential areas. Um, why do you think it is that some areas, some residential areas, are more pleasant to live in than others?

Candidate: More?

Examiner: More pleasant to live in.

Candidate: Er, because the er, residence, residential areas, is er, uh er, it's not, er, really it's not in Turkey, it's not, er, maybe it's, er, for, er, develop, developed countries, it's not, er, for developing countries, 'cause it's different. Um, actually we have no, er, we have no one centre, and we have no residence areas. All this you can go and see, you can stay.

Examiner: Right, but I guess is one area nicer than another area?

Candidate: Yeah.

Examiner: So what makes that area nicer?

Candidate: Ah nicer, er. It's yeah, it's, if it's near the centre, it's in, er, if it's, er, you can, er, get easily, er, transport, transportation, it's, er, and you can go everywhere. It's the centre like, um, it's the people prefer the like the safe areas.

Examiner: So, convenience?

Candidate: Yeah, convenience.

Examiner: Right, OK. Well, thank you very much. That's the end of the Speaking Test.

Candidate: Yeah, thank you.

See the answer key on pages 168–70 for an analysis of this candidate's performance.

SPEAKING
CD 3 · Track 3

Sample speaking test: Candidate 2

Examiner: Good afternoon. Could I have your full name, please?

Candidate: Good afternoon. My full name is Luo Xiaojing; that is my Chinese name.

Examiner: All right. And can I see your passport, please?

Candidate: OK. Here you are.

Examiner: Thank you. That's fine. Now, in the first part of the test, I'd like to ask you some questions about yourself. Ah, let's talk about what you do. Are you a student or do you have a job?

Candidate: Mm, I'm a student now. I have the language course is in Macquarie and then I will going to have the Master of Commerce.

Examiner: OK. And, er, why did you decide to do a Masters of Commerce?

Candidate: Mm. Um, because I think, if I can gain the Master degree maybe I will give a good job in China. And I will have a more opportunity, uh, to get a good pay job which is more appealing.

Examiner: All right. Um, later in life do you want to study something else?

Candidate: Sorry?

Examiner: Later in life do you want to study something else?

Candidate: Yes, of course. Cause I think study is, uh, is better to me and, uh, I think, uh, I ... I will continue my studies throughout my life.

Examiner: OK. Ah, now let's go on to the topic of reading magazines. Um, what kinds of magazines are popular in your country?

Candidate: Maybe the magazine about the superstars such as movie star, uh, TV star and, uh, the singer, the famous singer. Um, a lot of younger people like to see the magazine about it.

Examiner: Right. Um, why do some people prefer to read magazines rather than books?

Candidate: Mm. I think one of the reason is that in magazines, um, the people can see a lot of pictures then colourful and I think it's fantastic.

Examiner: OK. Can you learn much from magazines?

Candidate: Oh, something. You can gain some information about the magazine but I think, um, I will ... I will not spend a lot of time to see the magazine.

Examiner:	OK. Do you often read magazines?
Candidate:	No, not often.
Examiner:	Right, um, now I'd like to talk to you about drinks. Um, what are the most popular drinks in your country?
Candidate:	Beer, yeah.
Examiner:	Yeah, OK.
Candidate:	And, uh, maybe Coca-Cola, but I dislike it. I always drink the orangey water and, uh, just drink the water.
Examiner:	All right. Um, are there any drinks that people have at special times?
Candidate:	Mm, yeah, uh, I think maybe in the parties such as birthday party or any, uh, celebration kind of party, the people will drink a lot of such as, uh, beer and any alcohol, alcohol water. Yeah, alcohol drink, sorry.
Examiner:	Mm hm. All right. Um, are there any hot drinks you like?
Candidate:	No I don't like.
Examiner:	OK and, uh, what do you think are the healthiest drinks?
Candidate:	Mm. In my country a lot of people believe that, um, a little drink is better to your health, but I'm not sure because I think the men is always drink a lot and they cannot control, so I think drink is lot to their body.
Examiner:	Right. Now we have the second part of the Speaking Test. I'm going to give you a card about a topic, and I'd like you to talk about it for one to two minutes. Before you start, you can have one minute to think about what you are going to say, and if you want to, you can make some notes. Do you understand?
Candidate:	Yes.
Examiner:	All right. So here is some paper and a pencil for making notes, and here's your topic. I'd like you to describe a house or an apartment you've lived in and which you liked.

You can see the candidate's card for this speaking test on page 100.

Examiner:	All right? So remember, you can talk for one to two minutes. I'll tell you when the time is up. Could you start speaking now, please?
Candidate:	Yeah, now I will describe a house to you. Um, once I have been to Sydney I live in a big, very big house. The house has in Willoughby. You know Willoughby is quite far from the Macquarie and I like … I like the house very much because it's, it's very beautiful. The house is very big. There are six bedroom and two toilets, hm, a kitchen, a living room, uh, and a, a very big parking room. I think it's very big, um, because in, in China my apartment is quite small so I fe … I always fix stress when I live in it. Mm, ah, ah, after, after the courses I always go to, go to my house, I prefer to stay in my bedroom instead of go outside

because, uh, I have a little friend and I think, uh, the house is quite comfortable. Mm, uh, of, of course I have three, three housemate. Most of them come from China. We always chat but, uh, one of the problem is that we always chat with Chinese. I think that is not good enough to me. Uh, in a word I like the house and I think it's beautiful, clear, large and, uh, it's very comfortable, so I think it's better for me.

Examiner: So is that home similar to other places in the area?

Candidate: Sorry?

Examiner: Is that home similar to other places in the area?

Candidate: Mm, no, maybe not.

Examiner: OK. All right. Well thank you very much.

Candidate: Oh, thanks.

Examiner: You've been talking about a house or an apartment you have lived in, and now I want to discuss a few more general questions connected to this. Firstly, let's look at finding a place to live. Um, how do people usually find a place to live in your country?

Candidate: In my country, always go to the, uh, look for the advertisement and to gain some information about the house. Ah, maybe you, maybe the people can use a computer, um, collect the information from the Internet or buy some new newspaper, they always have some information about it. Ah, of course there are agents about just, uh, work for the, the rent, so I think it's quite easy for a person who want to have, who want to have, who want to have looking for a house.

Examiner: All right. So what factors do you think determine where people choose to live?

Candidate: Mm, I think most of, most of the important reason is comfortable and the price and the convenient. Yeah.

Examiner: Right. And, um, how would you compare, then, living in an apartment and living in a house?

Candidate: Mm, when I in China I live in the apartment, it's quite small, mm, and, ah, I will feel, um, it's not as comfortable as the house. However, uh, in my, in my a …, a …, sorry, apartment, I, I never find any insect because I live in the fifth floor of the building, the building quite high and, uh, higher world than when I lived in the house. Uh, sometime they can find the insect climbing to my house. I'm afraid of it.

Examiner: All right. Well, now let's look at home ownership. Um, do most people in your country rent their home or do they own their own home?

Candidate: Mm, if they have house or apartment, uh, most of people prefer to live in his own house because the, the rent of the house is quite expensive, especially in Shanghai and Beijing and in other big cities. Mm, I think the people should not put some money to rent a house if he had his own house. That's not economic.

Examiner: So what do you think is the difference in attitudes towards a house if you are a renter or you are an owner of that house? Do you think their attitudes towards their homes are different?

Candidate: Towards?

Examiner: Um, no, do you think an attitude of a renter, um, of a house compared to the attitude of an owner of the house is different?

Candidate: Oh, of course it's different. If I have my own house, I lived in it and I feel, oh, that it, that belongs to me. And I think I have a family, um, but if I live in the house just rent from somebody, I think I'm always worried maybe I will have to move another house.

Examiner: Right.

Candidate: I think that it quite different.

Examiner: So how does that affect how they treat the house?

Candidate: Mm, treat?

Examiner: Um, how, how they, um, how they treat that house. So, do you think that they think of the house in a better way or a worse way, if they are a renter?

Candidate: Yeah, uh, I think the people can compare with others. If I have rent a house and I lived it for a, for a long time, maybe I think, oh, it's OK to me, but when I look, um, with it to my friend, maybe I will find out that his house is better to me, so I will all think maybe I will have to looking for another house.

Examiner: OK. Lastly, let's look at residential areas. Um, do you think that it's better to live in the city or that it's better to live in a suburban area?

Candidate: Mm. I think the both benefit and, uh, disadvantages to live in the city or the countryside. Uh, in the city the life will become very convenient and it's very easy for you to go out for shopping and visit your friend and, uh, check bars to any place, but I think the, maybe the environment is not good enough and the traffic is bad too. If you want to go out or go to work, go to university, you'll find that the traffic always block, it will waste a lot of time. Mm. However, if the person live in countryside, uh, and the life is very leisure, but I think you maybe you will feel lonely. Yeah, nobody can try to reach you, nobody can tell, can take care of you. You just live by yourself, and maybe you just stay at home and watch the TV and, uh, call your friend. I think, uh, it's bad for the young people.

Examiner: OK. Well, thank you very much. That's the end of the Speaking Test.

Candidate: Thanks.

See the answer key on page 170–2 for an analysis of this candidate's performance.

SPEAKING

CD 3 · Track 4

Sample speaking test: Candidate 3

Examiner: Hello, could you tell me your full name please?

Candidate: Roby Sidhu.

Examiner: All right and can I see your passport?

Candidate: Here is my passport.

Examiner: OK, thank you. Now, in the first part of the test I'd like to ask you some questions about yourself. Let's talk about what you do. Uh, why did you decide to study English?

Candidate: Um, because uh in in this competition of us uh you need English if you are going, it helps in your career and I love to travel around the world so I think English is an international language so it will help me to communicate with people.

Examiner: OK. Is it an interesting subject to study?

Candidate: No, it's not interesting subject uh, because you have to just learn grammar and um, yes pretty boring it's not too interesting like er anything new.

Examiner: OK and do you have plans to do further study?

Candidate: Yeah I do, um actually I want to become um, uh nurse so I want to do that nursing course um, yeah I'm really into like um looking after people so I want to do this.

Examiner: OK now let's go on to the topic of reading magazines. What kinds of magazines are popular in your country?

Candidate: So, in India people love cricket so, the ... because nowadays Indian cricket players they're doing very well so, the people like to buy er cricket magazines and they're reading a lot about er Indian players, yeah.

Examiner: OK why do you think some people prefer to read magazines rather than books?

Candidate: Er in books like people have to spend a lot of time to get a idea what they reading about but in magazines they can get like er, er they can get an idea about the thing what they are reading about just in a shorter period, short period of time and in a sense like short look, quick look, yeah.

Examiner: Can you learn anything from magazines?

Candidate: Yeah, you can learn a lot from magazines like um er it tells about those other products and er ...

Examiner: OK that's fine, um. Now I'd like to talk to you about drinks. What are some of the most popular drinks in your country, India?

Candidate: In India actually I'm from Punjab, like so, we like er traditional dishes, drink is lassi so people love to drink that lassi so it's like very nice drink and you drink it um with ice and salt so it's very popular in India.

Examiner: OK are there any drinks that people have at special times?

Candidate: Yeah there's, there are some special drinks like some um, um, er homemade alcohol that people they make them er on the wedding parties. They make at home and the drink, it's really nice the people love um love that.

Examiner: OK are there any hot drinks that you like?

Candidate: Uh, I like hot drink like er hot chocolate. I really enjoy it just very dark chocolate, yeah.

Examiner: OK and finally what are the healthiest drinks, do you think?

Candidate: I think juices are the healthiest drinks and those are shakes like uh mango shake, banana shake with milk, these are the healthiest drinks.

Examiner: OK, um now Roby, we have the second part of the speaking test. I am going to give you a card about a topic and I'd like you to talk about it for one to two minutes. Before you start you have one minute to think about what you are going to say. If you want to, you can make some notes. Do you understand?

Candidate: Yeah, thank you.

Examiner: OK here's some paper and a pencil for making notes, and here's your topic. I'd like you to describe a house or an apartment you have lived in and which you liked. So, you have one minute to prepare.

Candidate: OK.

You can see the candidate's card for this speaking test on page 100.

Examiner: All right um remember you can talk for one to two minutes. I'll tell you when the time is up. Can you start speaking now, please?

Candidate: When I firstly came to Australia, so um, er, I lived in Springvale er it's just like er this is a very big house, three bedroom house, I really like it, it was in very like er um peaceful area and really neat and clean. So I used to live with my friends, so I had my own room, the house was like built with um timber floor and er painted white, white and blue, so these are my favourite colours. So my room was really big and the curtains were really nice and I had that um street view from my uh from my windows, I like that because there is a park on the next side of the street. So I can watch people playing football because I love football, and er it was near to all the facilities like hospital, library and um supermarket, and there is a park also as I just mentioned earlier, um so I love to play football it was very easy for me to just go there and just um I can just walk up for one minute and I can go there, and er we had a garden also, in the front and a backyard. So I love gardening also so I had a lot of flowers and veggies at my place, some home gardens. So the house was my favourite house in my whole life er until now. So I am still looking for a house, for that kind of house. So because I want to live in a very peaceful area – er just we had a one this one good thing of that house was like a separate toilet and separate wash room and separate um laundry, because in Australia, in Melbourne, mostly um mostly in Melbourne, you can't get er like different laundry facilities that was good thing about that house.

Examiner: All right, thank you Roby. You have been talking about a house or an apartment you have lived in and now I want you to discuss a few more general questions connected to this. Firstly, let's look at finding a place to live. How do people usually find a place to live in your country, India?

Candidate: Like other normal countries, in my country people also use those travel oh sorry, um those real estate agents. So these people are really helpful and they can find whatever they are looking for that's easy for them because they can tell them those people like what they are looking for and they will help to find those places and even on the other hand they can use the internet also, it is really helpful. So you can do it at home also you don't have to go and see someone else so you can find it very easily on the internet also.

Examiner: And what factors do you think determine where people choose to live?

Candidate: Like living around er um all those facilities like hospitals, library, um playgrounds and some other leisure activity centres and um dispensaries. So these kind of factors er I think determine, people should determine before er before living anywhere else.

Examiner: What is it like to live in an apartment compared to living in a house – do you think?

Candidate: Er living in a house is different than living in an apartment. So if you are living in a house, a house would be like very open side it would be big, more bigger than a apartment. So you can have a backyard also, a garden also, and you can you can't like, if you are living in a house you have a separate wall from your neighbours or you will have a gap between your house and the neighbour's house, so you can't hear the neighbour's cry so it will be more separate from the – from other houses. But living in er apartment is like er, um it's, living in an apartment also have some good qualities like er here it's more secure than living in a house um and you can have a view if you are living in an apartment. The building will be more taller than a house um – most stories, apartments – so you can have a view of city and area wherever you are living, and you can have er fresh air if you are living in an apartment.

Examiner: OK thanks, um let's now look at home ownership. So do most people rent their homes or own their homes where you're from?

Candidate: Er in my town people actually own their own place. So because it's very expensive renting a place in um my town because it's so, very industrial town so all those um migrant peoples are living there and it's very expensive to own uh to rent a place.

Examiner: OK, um could you compare the attitudes of someone who's renting a home and someone who owns their own home?

Candidate: People who er owns their own home. So they are very comfortable in their own place because the way you want things you can do whatever you want to do. The colour like colour-wise and picture-wise and the furniture-wise whatever you want to do, to your place you can do. If you are renting a place it's like you, you kind of feeling like you have to move soon and you can't do this, you can't do this you, even you can't paint your room like the colour you want and the pictures you want, you can't do that. And you have to look after the property a lot.

Examiner: So you're nervous if you rent a home?

Candidate: Yeah, I think so.

Examiner: OK, should the government help people to buy their own homes, do you think?

Candidate: Yeah in some like in developing countries the government should help those people who can't afford to buy a place um like um, mostly those people who are living below the line, the line of poverty, so government should help them to buy a place, the government financial and er, and um help them to get a job so they can buy, so they can afford to buy a place.

Examiner: Let's now look at residential areas. Why do you think some residential areas are more pleasant to live than others?

Candidate: Some residential areas are very like er very good than others so because they er they are near to all of the facilities whatever we need in our social life like er, er activity, leisure activity centres, libraries, schools, markets and a peaceful area and some parks those are the er, um basic needs of um human beings so we need that. Yeah, these places, these kinds of places are very comfortable than others.

Examiner: OK and finally, Roby, could you compare living in the centre of the city and in a suburban area?

Candidate: Living in the city is pretty congested so because the city is er, there is all those tall buildings and it's noisy and it can be a bit polluted also than suburban areas because suburban is more wider than city, you can have like a very peaceful um peaceful life in suburban areas and a bit more space so you can have your own garden and backyard, but in city if you are living in an apartment it is a bit hard to get all those things, yeah.

Examiner: OK, thanks very much Roby, that's the end of the speaking test.

Candidate: Thank you.

See the answer key on pages 172–4 for an analysis of this candidate's performance.

Speaking Test 1

CD 3 • Track 5

When you listen to the recording, after you hear each question you should press 'pause' and answer the question before going on to the next question.

Part 1 Introduction and interview

Hello. Could you say your full name, please?

And can I see your passport?

Thank you. Now, in the first part of the test, I'd like to ask you some questions about .yourself.

Let's talk about your work.

What job do you do?

When did you first think about doing this kind of work?

What do you like about your job?

Do you think you'll be working in this field in ten years' time?

Now let's talk about music.

What type of music did you like when you were a teenager?

Have you ever been to a live music concert?

At what times of day do you prefer to listen to music?

Do you often hear other people play music you don't like?

Next I'd like to talk about eating lunch.

What did you often eat for lunch when you were a school pupil?

Do you think lunch should be the main meal of the day?

Is it a good idea for people to have a rest after lunch?

Do you sometimes not have enough time for lunch?

Part 2 Individual long turn

Now we have the second part of the Speaking Test. I'm going to give you a card about a topic and I'd like you to talk about it for one to two minutes. Before you start, you can have one minute to think about what you are going to say. If you want to, you can make some notes. Do you understand? Here's some paper and a pencil for making notes and here's your topic.

I'd like you to describe a time when you complained about something you had paid for (for example, a restaurant meal, a product in a shop).

Describe a time when you complained about something you had paid for (e.g. a restaurant meal, a product in a shop).
You should say:

> why you complained
>
> how you complained
>
> whether it was useful to complain

and explain how you felt after you had complained.

All right? Remember you can talk for one to two minutes. I'll tell you when the time is up. Could you start speaking now, please?

Did you tell your friends about this?

Do people often complain about products and service in your country?

All right, thank you.

Part 3 Discussion

You've been talking about a time when you complained about something and now I want to discuss a few more general questions connected to this.

Firstly, let's talk about complaining.

What are some things people often complain about these days?

What is more effective – complaining by writing an email or by talking face to face with the person responsible?

Are there situations when it's better *not* to complain?

Now let's talk about being patient.

Could you describe some situations in daily life when people need to be patient?

Do you think technology such as email and mobile phones have made people less patient?

What are some benefits of being impatient?

Finally, let's talk about being satisfied in life.

Would you say most people are satisfied with their lives?

Do rich people tend to be more content than poor people?

Do you agree that, in general, humans tend to be dissatisfied rather than satisfied?

Thank you very much. That is the end of the Speaking Test.

Speaking Test 2

CD 3 • Track 6

When you listen to the recording, after you hear each question you should press 'pause' and answer the question before going on to the next question.

Part 1 Introduction and interview

Hello. Could you tell me your full name, please?

And can I see your passport?

Thank you. Now, in the first part of the test, I'm going to ask you some questions about yourself.

Let's talk about what you study.

What was the last course you studied?

Did anyone encourage you to choose that course?

What was more interesting for you – attending classes or reading course materials?

Are you happy that you chose that course?

Next, let's talk about visitors to your country.

Do many people from other countries visit your country?

Have you ever met any foreign tourists in your country?

How important is tourism to the economy of your country?

Do you think tourism will increase or decrease in the next few years?

Now I'd like to talk about watching movies.

What was the last film you saw?

How often do you watch the same movie again?

Do you prefer going to the cinema in the daytime or at night?

Would you watch a whole movie on a small screen such as an iPod?

Part 2 Individual long turn

Now we come to the second part of the Speaking Test. I'm going to give you a card about a topic and I'd like you to talk about it for one to two minutes. Before you start, you can have one minute to think about what you are going to say. If you want to, you can make some notes. Do you understand? Here's some paper and a pencil for making notes and here's your topic.

I'd like you to describe an occasion when you bought a special gift or present for someone.

Describe an occasion when you bought a special gift or present for someone.
You should say:

> what you bought
>
> where you bought it
>
> why you chose that present

and explain how you felt when you gave the present to the other person.

All right? Remember you can talk for one to two minutes. I'll tell you when the time is up. Could you start speaking now, please?

Would you like to receive a present like that yourself?

Do you like buying presents?

All right, thank you.

Part 3 Discussion

You've been talking about a time when you bought a special gift or present for someone and now I want to discuss a few more general questions connected to this.

Firstly, let's talk about giving presents.

When do people give presents in your culture?

What kind of presents do you think adults should give to children?

Is it ever acceptable to give money as a present?

Now let's talk about receiving presents.

What are some ways people show gratitude when they receive a present?

Is there anything people should avoid doing or saying when they receive a present in your country?

Are there any situations where a person should *not* accept a gift?

Finally, let's talk about why people give and receive presents.

Would you agree or disagree with the statement that 'people sometimes give expensive presents instead of spending time with a person'?

Do you agree that, when people give presents, they usually expect something in return?

Does giving and receiving presents sometimes have negative rather than positive results?

Thank you very much. That is the end of the Speaking Test.

Speaking Test 3

CD 3 • Track 7

When you listen to the recording, after you hear each question you should press 'pause' and answer the question before going on to the next question.

Part 1 Introduction and interview

Hello. Could you tell me your full name, please?

And can I see your passport?

Thank you. Now, in the first part of the test, I'm going to ask you some questions about yourself.

Let's talk about where you live.

What made you choose the place where you live now?

How long have you lived there?

Would you say it's a good area for families to live in?

Would it be a better area to live if there were fewer people than now?

Next, let's talk about how people pay for things they buy.

How do you prefer to pay for things that you buy, in cash or by card?

When you pay cash for something, do you usually check the change that you are given?

What is the most common way of paying for things in your country?

When you go to another country, do you have problems using a different currency?

Now I'd like to talk about getting up early in the morning.

Did you like to get up early in the morning when you were a child?

What are some advantages of getting up early?

Do you feel different at the beginning of the day than at the end of the day?

What do you think is the best time to get up in the morning?

Part 2 Individual long turn

Now we come to the second part of the Speaking Test. I'm going to give you a card about a topic and I'd like you to talk about it for one to two minutes. Before you start, you can have one minute to think about what you are going to say. If you want to, you can make some notes. Do you understand? Here's some paper and a pencil for making notes and here's your topic.

I'd like you to describe a website you have used.

Describe a website you have used.
You should say:
    how you found that website
    what that website is about
    how often you access it
and explain how you feel about that website.

All right? Remember you can talk for one to two minutes. I'll tell you when the time is up. Could you start speaking now, please?

Do you think that website could be improved?
Do you use the Internet a lot?

All right, thank you.

Part 3 Discussion

You've been talking about a website you have used and now I want to discuss a few more general questions connected to this.

Firstly, let's talk about using the Internet.

What are some of the main reasons people use the Internet in your country?

Could you compare looking for information on the Internet and in a book?

How do you think the Internet might change in the future?

Now let's talk about finding reliable information.

Do you think we can generally believe what we see on the Internet?

Where can we find the most reliable reports: on the Internet, on TV or in a newspaper?

How is it possible to check whether information you receive is correct or not?

Finally, let's talk about misuse of the Internet.

What are some ways people use the Internet to trick or deceive other people?

What can governments do to try to stop Internet fraud?

Do you think that misuse of the Internet will lead to less trust between strangers in the future?

Thank you very much. That is the end of the Speaking Test.

Speaking Test 4

CD 3 • Track 8

When you listen to the recording, after you hear each question you should press 'pause' and answer the question before going on to the next question.

Part 1 Introduction and interview

Hello. Could you tell me your full name, please?

And can I see your passport?

Thank you, that's fine. Now, in the first part of the test, I'd like to ask you some questions about yourself.

Let's talk about your job.

What do you do?

When did you first start doing that job?

Do you enjoy your work?

What are the people you work with like?

Now we'll look at the topic of dancing.

Is dancing very popular in your country?

Do you and your friends prefer to dance, or to watch other people dancing?

Are there special times when people like to dance?

Do you ever go dancing?

Let's now go on to the topic of computers.

Do you often use a computer?

How are computers most helpful?

Have you ever had a problem with a computer?

Do you think it'll be possible one day to have a conversation with a computer?

Part 2 Individual long turn

Now we have the second part of the Speaking Test. I'm going to give you a card about a topic and I'd like you to talk about it for one to two minutes. Before you start, you can have one minute to think about what you are going to say. If you want to, you can make some notes. Do you understand? Here's some paper and a pencil for making notes and here's your topic.

I'd like you to describe something interesting that you are going to do in your free time.

Describe something interesting that you are going to do in your free time.
You should say:

>   what it is

>   when you're going to do it

>   why it will be interesting

and explain how you feel about doing it.

All right? Remember you can talk for one to two minutes. I'll tell you when the time is up.
Could you start speaking now, please?

Have you ever done anything like this before?
Could anything prevent you from doing it?

All right, thank you.

Part 3 Discussion

You've been talking about something interesting you are going to do and now I want to discuss a few more general questions connected to this.

Firstly, let's look at making plans.

What are some things in life that people need to plan for carefully?

Are there any important things that people cannot prepare for?

Why do you think some people don't like making plans?

Now let's talk about hopes.

In your country, what are some things that many people hope to achieve in life?

Could you compare these with the hopes and ambitions people had when your parents were young?

Why do people need to have hopes and dreams?

Finally, let's talk about attitudes to the future.

Could you compare people who are optimistic and people who are pessimistic about the future?

How does a person's attitude to the future affect their life?

Do you think that people should be optimistic about the future of the world these days?

Thank you very much. That is the end of the Speaking Test.

Speaking Test 5

CD 3 • Track 9

When you listen to the recording, after you hear each question you should press 'pause' and answer the question before going on to the next question.

Part 1 Introduction and interview

Good afternoon. Could you tell me your full name, please?

And can I see your passport?

Thank you. Now, in the first part of the test, I'd like to ask you some questions about yourself.

Let's talk about where you live.

Could you describe the area where you live now?

How long have you lived there?

Why did you choose to live in that area?

What kind of people live in your area?

Now we'll talk about sleep.

How many hours a night do you think people need to sleep?

What do you do if you feel sleepy but you have to stay awake?

In your country, do people often have a sleep during the daytime?

How do you feel when you are woken by an alarm clock?

Now let's talk about watching television.

What kinds of TV programs do you like?

What time of day do you prefer to watch TV?

Have you ever lived in a home where there was no television?

Do you think people watch too much TV these days?

Part 2 Individual long turn

Now we come to the second part of the Speaking Test. I'm going to give you a card about a topic and I'd like you to talk about it for one to two minutes. Before you start, you can have one minute to think about what you are going to say. If you want to, you can make some notes. Do you understand? Here's some paper and a pencil for making notes and here's your topic.

I'd like you to describe a film you have seen that made an impression on you.

Describe a film you have seen that made an impression on you.
You should say:
> what it was about
> how popular it was
> what you thought about the actors
and explain why it made an impression on you.

All right? Remember you can talk for one to two minutes. I'll tell you when the time is up. Could you start speaking now, please?

When did you last see that film?
Do you often watch films?

All right, thank you.

Part 3 Discussion

You've been talking about a film you have seen that made an impression on you and now I want to discuss a few more general questions connected to this.

Firstly, let's look at the importance of entertainment.

What kinds of entertainment are popular in your country?

Could you compare types of entertainment children like and adults like?

Why is entertainment important in people's lives?

Now let's talk about famous actors.

Why do you think people are interested in the private lives of famous actors?

In your opinion, is the amount of money earned by film stars justified?

What would it be like to be a famous actor?

Finally, let's talk about global culture.

How much influence does American culture have in your country?

What are Hollywood films like in comparison with films produced in your country?

How can a country avoid being dominated by a foreign culture?

Thank you very much. That is the end of the Speaking Test.

Speaking Test 6

CD 3 • Track 10

When you listen to the recording, after you hear each question you should press 'pause' and answer the question before going on to the next question.

Part 1 Introduction and interview

Hello. Could you tell me your full name, please?

And can I see your passport?

Thank you. Now, in the first part of the test, I'd like to ask you some questions about yourself.

Let's talk about where you come from.

Which country do you come from?

What's the best time of year to visit your country?

Are many different languages spoken in your country?

Are there any areas in your country where very few people live?

Now, let's move on to talk about light.

Do you prefer buildings with a lot of light or ones with a more shaded style?

How do you feel working or studying in a room without windows?

Do you think very bright advertising signs at night are a good idea?

Could you live without electric lights at home?

Let's go on to talk about visiting people.

Do people often visit friends in their homes in your country?

At what times or on what days do people usually visit friends?

Should you tell people you are coming before visiting them at home?

Do people ever take presents when visiting friends in your country?

Part 2 Individual long turn

Now we come to the second part of the Speaking Test. I'm going to give you a card about a topic and I'd like you to talk about it for one to two minutes. Before you start, you can have one minute to think about what you are going to say. If you want to, you can make some notes. Do you understand? Here's some paper and a pencil for making notes and here's your topic.

I'd like you to describe a river, lake or beach that you know.

Describe a river, lake or beach that you know.

You should say:

>>> where it is

>>> what it looks like

>>> what people use it for

and explain whether you like it or not.

All right. Remember you can talk for one to two minutes. I'll tell you when the time is up. Could you start speaking now, please?

Do you often go to that place?

Is it a popular place for leisure activities?

All right, thank you.

Part 3 Discussion

You've been talking about a river, lake or beach that you know and now I want to ask you a few more general questions connected to this.

Firstly, let's look at holidays near water.

Could you tell me about some places near water where people like to take holidays in your country?

What are some activities people can do when they have a holiday near water?

Why do you think people often find it relaxing to be near water?

Now we'll talk about transport on water.

How important is water transportation these days?

Could you compare travelling on water and travel by road?

In the future, how important do you think travel by water will be?

And finally, let's consider water pollution.

What are some of the causes of water pollution?

What can governments do to prevent water being polluted?

What would happen if there were a global shortage of clean water?

Thank you very much. That is the end of the Speaking Test.

Transcripts

In these listening transcripts, the words that are <u>underlined</u> indicate where the answers to the questions can be found.

Listening Test 1

You will hear four different recordings and you will have to answer questions on what you hear.

There will be time for you to read the instructions and questions before the recording is played.

You will also have the opportunity to check your answers.

The recordings will be played ONCE only.

The test is in four sections. Write your answers on the question sheet as you listen. At the end of Section 4, you have ten minutes to transfer your answers onto the answer sheet, which is on page 31. When you finish, check the answers at the back of the book.

Now turn to Section 1.

Section 1

You will hear a telephone conversation between a woman who will soon move house and an employee of a telephone company.

First, you have some time to look at questions 1 to 5.

Now listen and answer questions 1 to 5.

Dan: Atlantic Telephone Company, my name is Dan. How can I help you?

Penny: Oh, hello, I'm calling because you're my telephone service provider and I'm going to be moving house next week. I need to have my phone disconnected and then I want to have it connected at the new address.

Dan: We can do that for you now over the phone, if you like.

Penny: Oh, that'd be good.

Dan: All right then. First, could you tell me your phone number?

Penny: Yes, it's 5062 7840.

The customer says the number is 5062 7840, so '5062 7840' has been written next to the example on the question paper. Now continue with questions 1 to 5.

Dan: Thank you. And is the account in your name?

Penny: Uh, yes, it is.

Dan: Could you spell your full name, please?

Penny: It's <u>Penny Ryan</u>, that's P-e-n-n-y ... R-y-a-n.

Dan: Thank you. Now, I just need to ask you a question for security purposes. I hope you don't mind, but could you tell me your date of birth, Ms Ryan?

Penny: No, I don't mind. It's the <u>24th of March 1982</u>.

Dan: Right. And do you know yet the date on which you'll be moving?

Penny: Yes, it's next Tuesday, the 16th of September.

Dan: Thank you. Now, madam, can you tell me where you'll be moving to?

Penny: My new address will be 18 King Street, <u>Blacktown</u>.

Dan: Uh-huh. I can allocate you a new telephone number now if you like, though it won't be operational till you actually have it connected.

Penny: That'd be really useful – I could tell my friends the new number even before I move.

Dan: Do you have a pen and paper handy?

Penny: Yes.

Dan: OK, your new number will be <u>7690 3275</u>.

Penny: Great.

Dan: Now, up until now you've been receiving your telephone bills once a month. As a long-standing customer, you have the option of being billed only once every three months if you like.

Penny: Oh, I'll stick with monthly bills, it just makes it easier for me to stay within my household budget.

Dan: All right then.

Before you hear the rest of the conversation, you have some time to look at questions 6 to 10.

Now listen and answer questions 6 to 10.

Dan: Now, Ms Ryan, could you tell me which type of contract you are on with Atlantic Telephone Company? Is it Home Plus, Economy Saver or Flexible Bundle?

Penny: Oh, let me think. I think I used to be on Home Plus, but then I got a mobile phone and I wasn't using my landline that much anymore, so I switched plans. That's right, I switched to Economy Saver about a year ago.

Dan: Right, thank you. Now, I'd like to tell you about a new type of contract we have. It's called the Three-In-One. If you have your landline, your mobile and the Internet connection with us, you get a 20% discount every time you pay the bill.

Penny: Oh, but with my mobile I'm using a very cheap provider, but they're not that reliable. If I do switch contracts, will I be locked in for a certain time period?

Dan: Well, that's the case with Home Plus, but with this one you're free to change again at any time without penalty.

Penny: Oh, in that case I'll switch from Economy Saver to Three-In-One.

Dan: Good. I'm sure you'll find you make real savings with that.

Penny: Oh, I just have a question about the Internet.

Dan: Yes, what do you want to know?

Penny: There are certain times when I can make unlimited downloads, like if I want to download a movie. That's from 10 pm to 6 am, isn't it?

Dan: It's a bit more restricted than that, it's from 1 am to 6 am. It turns out that the peak period of accessing large files is from 11 at night to 2 in the morning.

Penny: Oh, that's interesting, there must be a lot of night owls.

Dan: I suppose so. Now, do you mind if I ask you what's the main type of phone call you make? Any information you give me will be kept confidential, it's just information that helps us provide a better service to our customers.

Penny: Alright then, but what do you mean by 'type of phone call'?

Dan: Would you say the majority of your calls are to friends and relatives, or are they work-related, or for paying bills and so on?

Penny: Well, I started to work from home last year, so most of them were work-related, but then I didn't make enough money from that line of work, so I got a part-time job and now I mainly use the phone to call relatives. I tend to keep in contact with friends by email.

Dan: OK, thank you. Now just one more question then we'll be finished. In the years that you've been with Atlantic Telephone Company, how would you rate our service overall?

Penny: Well, initially there were a few problems, and it wasn't really satisfactory, but in general I'd say things have been mostly satisfactory. My previous service provider was very good, but they went bankrupt.

Dan: All right then, that wraps it up. Thank you very much and I hope your move goes smoothly.

Penny: Thank you.

That is the end of Section 1. You now have half a minute to check your answers.

Now turn to Section 2.

Section 2

A group of people has just arrived at their hotel for a two-week holiday. The hotel manager is talking to them about some hotel facilities and rules. First, you have some time to look at questions 11 to 17.

Now listen and answer questions 11 to 17.

Welcome, everyone, it's nice to see all of you here. I'd like to tell you a bit about the hotel, including a few 'dos' and 'don'ts'. I know you've just had a long trip, so I'll keep it brief so that you can go to your rooms and put your feet up.

We want you to relax and enjoy the casual atmosphere of this place – you *are* on holidays, after all – but I'd ask you not to walk around in bare feet, it's just that it's so easy to bring sand into the building when you come back from the beach, so we'd appreciate it if you could at least <u>wear shoes while on the premises</u>. Oh, and if you want to hire some equipment, you'll find a good range of gear such as beach umbrellas, surfboards and snorkelling equipment down at the <u>beach cafe</u> for quite reasonable rates. We used to hire out such things from reception, but that was discontinued last year.

If you do need to speak to someone at reception, there are staff on duty there seven days a week, usually either myself, Maureen or Bruce. The early risers among you might like to go down to the beach to see the sun rise at 6 o'clock, but we're <u>not open till seven in the morning and we're here until six in the evening</u>. You'll also find a range of brochures about activities and attractions in the district. If you need to contact hotel staff after hours, you can just call 7946 from the phone in your room. The cleaners come in to vacuum the rooms and clean the bathrooms every second day, and the bed sheets and towels are changed <u>twice a week, on Tuesdays and Fridays</u>.

Smoking is not allowed inside the building and we'd also ask you to refrain from smoking when you're near the swimming pool area. If you do need to have a cigarette, you can go out <u>onto your balcony</u>, where you'll also find an ashtray. When you're sitting out on your balcony, you might get a visit from some of the local <u>birds</u>. They're very colourful and friendly, but we'd ask you to resist the temptation to give them something to eat because they can quickly become dependent on handouts. There's a pond in the garden at the back of the hotel and we'd appreciate it if you didn't feed the <u>fish</u> – they can get quite ill unless they're given the right kind of food. Just one point on noise – there's a general house rule to keep noise to a minimum <u>after 11 at night</u>. It's fine to enjoy music and lively conversation, but it's important to be considerate and respect everyone's right to have a good sleep.

You now have some time to look at questions 18 to 20.

Now listen and answer questions 18 to 20.

I didn't mean to take up so much of your time, but I've just remembered that I need to tell you a few things about the disposal of garbage. We do like to do things in an environmentally friendly manner around here, and so we recycle garbage where possible. There are separate bins for glass and metal but we don't yet have a facility in this area for the recycling of plastic, so that should just go in with your general unrecyclable waste along with food scraps. The gardener wishes he could use them to make compost for the garden, but that's a little impractical at present. It'd be good if you could leave your old newspapers at reception – the local school is involved in a recycling project and they send someone to the hotel to pick them up.

If it's raining and you don't feel like going out, there are plenty of ways to pass the time in the hotel. There's a gym on the second floor if you want to get some exercise and a couple of billiard tables in a room next to the gym. For relaxation, there's a coin-operated spa, which is also located on the second floor. If you'd like to watch a movie, you can borrow a DVD from reception and watch it in your room. Also, if you've brought your laptop with you, you can connect to the Internet in your room for a small fee.

All these rules are designed to ensure you have a pleasant stay here. If any of you has the energy to go out tonight, you'll find there's plenty to do. Just around the corner there's a nightclub if you feel like some dancing, but if you want to have a few drinks without the music, there's a bar in the centre of town, but you'll need to take a taxi to get there. There's also a cinema and even a casino down there. If you like to sing, you'll find a karaoke club right across the road from the hotel. Anyway, I hope you all have a very happy stay with us.

That is the end of Section 2. You now have half a minute to check your answers.

Now turn to Section 3.

Section 3

You will hear a discussion between a nursing student and a tutor after the student has done some practical training at a home nursing service for older patients. First, you will have

some time to look at questions 21 to 26.

Now listen and answer questions 21 to 26.

Tutor: Now, you spent last week doing practical training with the home nursing service dealing with elderly patients. How did it go?

Student: Oh, it was pretty good. I mean, I learnt a lot since I hadn't had much to do with older patients before.

Tutor: Well, with our ageing population, care of the elderly is a major focus of the healthcare system, and quite a range of healthcare professionals are called upon.

Student: Yes, I was surprised in a few cases. For instance, we know that preventing falls is very important. There's a separate falls clinic, but if a patient appears to be unsteady on their feet, whether they're walking unaided or using a walking stick or a frame, the nurse has to get in touch with a physiotherapist.

Tutor: That's right. We always need to be on the lookout for signs of deteriorating health. If you notice that a patient is becoming disoriented, it could be caused by tiredness or the side effects of medication. So what you have to do is contact their doctor, who will then assess what the cause could be.

Student: Yeah. Sometimes it's hard to work out exactly what's wrong. There was one patient who bumped into furniture a few times in her own living room while we were there.

Tutor: Well, as you know, our vision can deteriorate with age, and in the case of elderly patients, we need to refer them to an occupational therapist if they're experiencing problems due to visual impairment. If necessary, it's up to that specialist to refer them to an optometrist.

Student: I see. What about the patients who don't want our help? I mean, they're free to live their lives as they want and we can't force them to see a doctor or someone.

Tutor: Yes, it's not unusual for our patients to <u>decline assistance</u>, especially the men. It's often a matter of pride or an overestimation of their own capabilities. But when there are potentially serious issues that could have a long-term impact on their health and safety, we get the <u>aged care team</u> to pay them a visit. Sometimes they just end up having a friendly chat, but at least they're informed about what services are available.

Student: So they provide a bit of psychological help, like a doctor often does. What about when a patient appears to be becoming increasingly <u>frail</u>? I mean, there could be a whole number of causes like the time of day or just simply old age.

Tutor: You need to remember that sometimes elderly patients can't go shopping regularly, or they can't afford much nutritious food. Because it can be a mixture of reasons that might need to be addressed by their doctor or the aged care team, we first contact a <u>dietician</u> because we find that almost everyone can benefit from an expert review of the types of food they're eating.

Student: What about the patients who have pets? I mean, I've been into some people's homes and they seem to be a kind of health hazard, especially the ones with a lot of cats, or birds in cages.

Tutor: Well, <u>pets</u> do a lot of good for humans – they provide company, they're a reason to get some exercise, particularly dogs, and generally they do more good than harm. But you're right, they can spread disease and also dogs and cats can trip up their owners. We used to let the occupational therapist handle that issue, but now if we have concerns, we give the <u>falls clinic</u> a call for a home assessment.

Student: Oh right, I'll just make a note about that.

Before you hear the rest of the conversation, you have some time to look at questions 27 to 30.

Now listen and answer questions 27 to 30.

Student: Some of the patients we visited last week had dementia, so I'd just like to clarify a few things about that if you don't mind.

Tutor: No, that's fine. With increasing life expectancy we're going to be seeing more and more of it.

Student: I know that dementia can be caused by genetic or environmental factors, such as over-indulging in alcohol over a long period of time, but it seems that it can be difficult to diagnose dementia because its symptoms can occur with various other conditions.

Tutor: That's right. Some of them, such as Pick's disease, can't be overcome, whereas others, such as <u>brain tumours, can</u>.

Student: One of the patients we saw appeared to be very <u>anxious</u>. I thought that might've been a side effect of the medication she was on, but the nurse I was training with told me it was a frequently occurring syndrome of people with dementia. They're <u>upset at not being able to do some of the things they could in the past and often don't trust those around them</u>.

Tutor: And many healthy people get anxious about the future, whether it's about things going on in their own lives or what's happening in the wider world. It's good though – one of life's pleasures that people with dementia continue to enjoy is food. Generally we find they're keen on cakes and desserts, so you have to make sure they have a balanced diet overall. Elderly people with dentures may avoid chewy food, and their taste receptors for salt can become diminished, which is a normal part of ageing.

Student: We had some lectures last month about research done on therapies to enhance the well-being of all kinds of age groups. For example, they told us that children recovering from surgery really like to sing if they've got the energy, people with dementia usually experience a lift in their mood while listening to music, and people with depression nearly always benefit from doing regular exercise.

Tutor: Yes, it's very rewarding to see patients responding to measures like those and it helps us view their health from a broader perspective.

That is the end of Section 3. You now have half a minute to check your answers.

Now turn to Section 4.

Section 4

You will hear a lecture to anthropology students about an ethnic group called the Tuareg. Many of these people live in the Sahara desert in Africa. First, you have some time to look at questions 31 to 40.

Now listen and answer questions 31 to 40.

Good afternoon, everyone. In today's lecture I'll be outlining some of the main economic activities of the Tuareg. The Tuareg are an ethnic group who live in north and west Africa, mostly in the Sahara desert and surrounding regions. There is no consensus on the size of the Tuareg population today, with most estimates ranging between 750,000 and 1.3 million people. The main reason for this uncertainty is their nomadic lifestyle; it's always difficult to conduct a census among people who do not live in permanent settlements. The Sahara is known around the world as a very arid region, and the ability of these people to survive in such an inhospitable environment is amazing. The Tuareg have sometimes been referred to as 'the blue people' because the indigo dye that is used to colour their clothing often comes off on their skin, giving it a blue colouring. Their staple diet consists of millet, a grain that they use to make porridge, as well as rice, wheat and other grains. In the dry season their staple foods are grain and dates, whereas in the cooler, wet season they have more milk and meat.

These days most Tuareg living in rural areas pursue a range of activities. These include the herding and breeding of livestock, carrying out gardening in the oases, and of course trade, which they have conducted for millennia. For more than 2,000 years they have operated camel caravans – these are groups of camels that carry goods over long distances, trading products between the Sahel region south of the Sahara up to the Mediterranean Sea on the coast of north Africa. The camel caravans, sometimes consisting of more than 20,000 camels, dominated trans-Saharan trade until the middle of the 20th century. A strong camel can carry up to a total of 300 kilograms of goods, excluding the rider. These caravans often cross the Sahara to the Sahel region to the south. At first the pace is slow to allow the camels to feed, but as they enter the barren desert where there is nothing to eat, they walk from morning to night, typically covering 50 kilometres in a day. In the semiarid Sahel region, which receives between 10 and 50 centimetres of rainfall per year, the Tuareg obtain cloth as well as millet grown by the Hausa people. In exchange for these, the Tuareg give them a number of products, in particular <u>salt and dates</u>. Although camels are still used, these days goods are more often carried by truck and train.

The Tuareg also grow some of their own food. Crops grown by the Tuareg include millet, barley, wheat, maize, onions, tomatoes and dates. In farming, there is a division of labour based on gender, with the men planting and irrigating the gardens, and <u>the women harvesting the crops</u>. Herding animals is also an important economic activity. The livestock Tuareg particularly value are camels and cattle rather than the smaller animals such as goats. In regard to herding animals, men usually take care of the camels, while <u>the women look after the goats</u>, sheep <u>and donkeys</u>.

For more than 1,000 years the Tuareg have been involved in the salt trade. The salt is obtained by digging pits 6 to 8 metres deep to reach water with a very high salt content, also known as brine. The summer heat evaporates the water, leaving the salt behind. The salt is then formed into blocks, which weigh around 21 kilograms, and packed into the hollowed-out trunks of palm trees. These are then wrapped in straw and loaded onto camels to be traded elsewhere. <u>The price of salt rises with the approach of summer because this is the time of year when animals need it most</u>. The best quality salt is used for human consumption, and the lower quality salt is given to animals.

One group among the Tuareg that is not involved in the camel caravans and farming are the <u>craftsmen</u> who make the distinctive jewellery and handicrafts. Traditionally they <u>had lower status due to their more sedentary lifestyle</u> – the Tuareg have always prized and enjoyed the freedom of a nomadic way of life, whereas the craftsmen need to stay in one place with their tools and workshops. However, for this same reason they were always able to gain a higher level of education than other Tuareg groups. With gradual modernisation, their higher education levels have come to be of more benefit to them, in addition to which their jewellery and leather goods have found a market among visitors from abroad.

The economic power of the Tuareg has deteriorated since countries in the region gained their independence in the 1960s and under the impact of severe droughts. Though most Tuareg continue to live as nomads, their traditional way of life is undergoing significant change.

That is the end of Section 4. You now have half a minute to check your answers.

That is the end of the Listening Test. You now have ten minutes to transfer your answers to the answer sheet.

Listening Test 2

You will hear four different recordings and you will have to answer questions on what you hear.

There will be time for you to read the instructions and questions before the recording is played.

You will also have the opportunity to check your answers.

The recordings will be played ONCE only.

The test is in four sections. Write your answers on the question sheet as you listen. At the end of Section 4, you have ten minutes to transfer your answers onto the answer sheet, which is on page 31. When you finish, check the answers at the back of the book.

Now turn to Section 1.

Section 1

You will hear a woman who is applying for a driving licence. First, you have some time to look at questions 1 to 5.

Now listen and answer questions 1 to 5.

Man: Good morning, can I help you?

Woman: I'd like to apply for a driving licence.

Man: Right. We'll just have to fill in this form.

Woman: Uh-huh.

Man: First, er, could you tell me your full name?

Woman: Yes, it's Theresa Collins.

Man: Right.

The woman says her name is Theresa Collins, so 'Theresa Collins' has been written next to the example on the question paper. Now continue with questions 1 to 5.

Man: And what type of vehicle would you like to drive?

Woman: Oh, just a normal car.

Man: That's a Class C licence then. And have you ever held a driving licence in another country?

Woman: Oh no, I'm too young. Anyway, I think I'd be too scared to drive in another country.

Man: Right. I'll just need to get some personal details from you. Um, could I have your date of birth, please?

Woman: Yes, it's the 17th of March 1994.

Man: And what's your address?

Woman: 28 River Street.

Man: That's spelt R-i-v-e-r, is that right?

Woman: Yes.

Man: And that's in Bentley, isn't it?

Woman: Yes.

Man: OK. And your phone number?

Woman: I'll give you my home number. It's 3701 8699.

Man: Right. And what form of ID do you have with you?

Woman: Well, I've got a bank card. Here it is.

Man: Let's see. No, we need something with your photo on it, like a student card.

Woman: I've got that with me, here you are.

Man: Yeah, that's fine. Now, there's an application fee of $55. How would you like to pay? We take credit cards but not cheques, I'm afraid. And we take cash of course, if you have enough money with you.

Woman: I do actually, and I try not to use my credit card if I can avoid it. Here you are.

Man: Thank you.

Before you hear the rest of the conversation, you have some time to look at questions 6 to 10.

Now listen and answer questions 6 to 10.

Man: Right, now there are a few things I need to tell you about the licence. Before you actually drive a car, you have to pass a test about the road rules.

Woman: Oh, that's the test about speed limits and road signs and things like that, isn't it?

Man: Yes, that's right. There are two parts to the test, and you're allowed to make a maximum of two errors in each section, so that's four altogether.

Woman: And if I fail the test, can I do it again?

Man: Yes you can, but you have to wait at least a week.

Woman: Right. And when I'm driving, <u>there's got to be someone with me in the car who holds a full licence</u>, doesn't there?

Man: Yes. That could be a family member, a professional driving instructor or a friend.

Woman: What about my older sister?

Man: Sure, as long as she's got the right kind of licence. Now the learner's licence is valid for nine months. At the end of that time you have to do a practical driving test. If you pass that, you're granted a provisional licence. That <u>expires after 18 months</u>. If you don't pass the practical driving test, you are given a learner's licence for another six months.

Woman: I see. And while I'm still on the learner's licence, how fast can I drive?

Man: Well, it depends on the area you're driving in. In most places in the city, there's a speed limit of 60 kilometres an hour. As you probably know, on highways in the countryside there's often a speed limit of 100 kilometres per hour. But as a learner <u>you're never allowed to exceed 80</u>, even on a highway.

Woman: Right. I think that'd be fast enough for me anyway.

Man: Is there anything else you need to know?

Woman: Oh yeah, I heard there are restrictions on using mobile phones while you're driving.

Man: That's right. Until recently, you could only talk on a mobile while you're driving if you used an earphone or hands-free device, but that's been changed.

Woman: Oh?

Man: Yeah. Now <u>you can't use mobiles at all while driving</u>.

Woman: Not even to send an SMS?

Man: Not even to send an SMS. Anyway, if that's all, I'll give you a copy of the book on the road rules.

Woman: Thanks very much.

You now have half a minute to check your answers.

Now turn to Section 2.

Section 2

You will hear a training officer giving a talk to new staff who will be working at the information desk at an airport. First, you have some time to look at questions 11 to 15.

Now listen and answer questions 11 to 15.

Now, when you're working at the information desk in the arrivals section of the airport, one of the most common questions people ask is, what's the best way to get to their hotel or to a particular address once they leave the airport. The answer you give them depends on a number of factors, so I'm going to give you a few general tips to help you deal with these issues by taking the case of a typical destination for the average traveller.

After a long flight, people are often tired and want to get to their final destination as soon as possible. You'd think that the <u>quickest way</u> would be to take a taxi, but because of traffic congestion, it turns out that it's usually better to <u>take the train</u>. Trains are cheaper than taxis, and taxis get caught in traffic jams and they can't go through red lights. For some passengers, the most important consideration is to take a means of transport that is going to run according to schedule. Now, you would think that the train would be the best one for this, but as the airport train is operated by a private company, there have been a lot of problems integrating its running times with the publicly owned train network, and this has resulted in a lot of delays. Surveys on travelling to and from the airport have found that <u>minibuses are the most dependable form of transport</u>.

There are other considerations too. If a person wants <u>a comfortable ride</u> with plenty of legroom after a long flight in a cramped seat, it'd be best for them to take one of the large, air-conditioned <u>buses</u>. It's a new fleet with plenty of space for luggage and, on top of that, they're much cheaper than taxis. Some passengers are far more concerned about <u>security</u>; of course we can't guarantee that they won't be robbed or even cheated by a dishonest driver, so I think for them the best thing to do is to get someone who they know and trust to pick them up in <u>their car</u>. Finally, there's also the 'green' traveller who wants to cause the <u>least possible pollution</u>. Now, obviously we can't tell them to walk because it's too far, particularly with heavy luggage. You might guess that public transport would be the cleanest way to travel, but it turns out that it's <u>taxis</u>, and that's because of the type of fuel they use. They're also not surprisingly the most popular choice of businesspeople.

You now have 30 seconds to look at questions 16 to 20.

Now listen and answer questions 16 to 20.

So far we've been focusing on the arrivals section of the airport. Now we're going to be looking at the departures section. You've all got a copy of the floor plan of the departures section of the airport. Because of the recent renovations, a lot of people are disoriented when they see it for the first time, so you need to be familiar with the new layout. At the bottom of the floor plan you can see where the passengers check in. They then go through security control and in front of them is the information desk, right in the middle of the whole floor plan. Just <u>to the right of the information desk there's a newsagency</u> where you can buy newspapers and magazines. For those who like to do a bit of shopping, to the left of the information desk we have a jewellery store – it's well worth a look at – and a well-stocked electronics goods shop, and <u>between those two there is a pharmacy</u>. There used to be a dress shop in that position. At the top right-hand corner of the diagram we have the waiting lounge and the exit to the planes.

In the top left-hand corner <u>are the public toilets</u>. You can use those toilets or, if you like, there are also staff facilities near the bookshop, but you'll need to get the key. Just behind the information desk we have some food outlets and over <u>to the right, next to the waiting lounge, is a cafe</u>. When the renovations are completed it will function as an Internet cafe. At most airports you get people congregating on the footpath smoking, which is unpleasant for the non-smokers entering and leaving the building. For that reason we've set up a <u>dedicated smoking room inside the terminal, next to the bookshop</u>. It's well ventilated and looks out onto the tarmac. The original plan was to put a wine bar next to the bookshop, but there were problems with the licensing laws.

I'd encourage you to walk around the airport to familiarise yourselves with the layout so that you can more easily handle passengers' enquiries.

That is the end of Section 2. You now have half a minute to check your answers.

Now turn to Section 3.

Section 3

You will hear two college students reporting to their science class about a project they have done on an Australian animal called the Tasmanian devil. First, you have some time to look at questions 21 to 26.

Now listen and answer questions 21 to 26.

Woman: Hi, everyone. For our assignment on a native animal, George and I chose that unusual Australian creature, the Tasmanian devil.

Man: Yeah. Actually, they don't deserve to be called 'devils', though they do have some strange habits.

Woman: Anyway, as their name indicates, they're only found in the wild on the island of Tasmania. You can find them all over the island, including in the south-west rainforests and in coastal heath areas, but they're most commonly found in the forests where there's less rainfall, in the eastern and northern parts of the island.

Man: In fact, they live any place where they can get shelter during the day and food at night.

Woman: Some of you may have seen one in a zoo. They're about the size of a small dog and are covered with short, soft, black fur with white markings on some parts of their bodies. An adult male can weigh from 5 to 13 kilograms, and a female from 4.5 to 9 kilograms.

Man: They've got a large head and neck, with heavy limbs. They're called devils because of the terrible sounds they make at night. This has given them an undeserved reputation for being aggressive, whereas in fact they're fairly shy creatures, but this doesn't mean that they're tame or friendly enough to be pets.

Woman: And like kangaroos, they carry their young in a pouch. They have babies only once a year, and then about 20 are born at one time, but at that stage they're only as big as a grain of rice. The babies have a race to the pouch, because there are only four teats there, and the mothers rear an average of three young annually.

Man: The babies stay in the pouch for about five months. Then they're left in their nest or are carried on their mother's back when she goes out, and eventually they have to look after themselves at about eight months. Then they in turn start breeding at the end of their second year.

Woman: And around 60% of them die in their first summer due to the tough competition for food. The ones that survive can live for up to seven years, which means they don't live as long as the average domestic dog.

Man: No. And it's estimated that now there are between 100,000 and 150,000 of them altogether. They were almost wiped out by the early European settlers because they hated the devils eating their chickens, so the government paid people to kill Tasmanian devils.

Woman: And most farmers still dislike them. Their numbers fell so drastically due to farmers poisoning them or shooting them that it was thought that they might have become extinct. Then a law was passed in 1941 to protect them, and since then their numbers have grown again.

Before you hear the rest of the talk, you have some time to look at questions 27 to 30.

Now listen and answer questions 27 to 30.

Man: Now we'd like to talk about some of their habits. They live alone in places such as hollow logs, caves or in burrows underground, which they line with bark, grass and leaves. They usually move slowly and look clumsy when they move quickly, but the young ones are more agile and can even climb trees.

Woman: But one of the most amazing things about Tasmanian devils is how and what they eat. They've got incredibly strong teeth and jaws, so a large male can give you a bite as strong as a 50-kilogram dog!

Man: But don't worry, they don't eat people! Some farmers complain about them taking young lambs, but their diet consists predominantly of animals that have already died. They don't get ill when they eat sick animals because of the digestive enzymes in their own stomachs that kill the diseases.

Woman: And they've got an undeserved reputation for being smelly, whereas in fact they wash themselves as much as cats do. They're nocturnal animals, so they go hunting at night, often travelling up to 15 kilometres and using their strong sense of smell to find food. They eat all kinds of animals – and they eat everything, including fur, and leave nothing behind except the largest bones.

Man: Yeah, there can be up to 22 of them feeding off one carcass at the same time, and they're very greedy, noisy eaters. In all the excitement of eating, there's a lot of coughing, barking and so on. It's quite common for them to bite each other to decide who can eat first, who goes second and so on.

Woman: And they've got an incredible appetite. They can eat the equivalent of 40% of their own body weight in just half an hour, which is like a human eating about 25 kilograms of steak. And they make really good use of their strong, blunt teeth. When they're frightened, they show them by yawning, which is more effective than biting or barking.

Man: But the only serious fighting that takes place is when they're looking for a mate. All in all, they're a fascinating little animal.

That is the end of Section 3. You now have half a minute to check your answers.

Now turn to Section 4.

Section 4

You will hear a lecture by a healthcare researcher to students of health science about the results of a survey on yoga in Australia. First, you have some time to look at questions 31 to 40.

Now listen and answer questions 31 to 40.

Good afternoon everyone. In today's lecture I'm going to present some of the findings of the largest and most comprehensive survey of yoga practice ever conducted in Australia. The objectives of this survey were to investigate the characteristics of people who practise yoga in this country, ah the styles and techniques of yoga that are practised, how often people practise yoga, the reasons why they do yoga and the perceived benefits of yoga practice. It is our hope that the findings of this survey will be of help to both teachers and students of yoga in this country and abroad, as well as to healthcare practitioners. Prior to our study, no nationwide research had been conducted into the topic. Our research team decided to do a web-based survey so that we would reach the maximum possible number of people all around the country, and also due to our funding limitations. The survey was promoted through yoga schools, the media and by word of mouth. Eventually, ah almost 4,000 people responded to the survey, which took about 30 minutes to complete. About one-third of the people who filled in the survey were yoga teachers, the other two-thirds were yoga students; overall, 85% of the respondents were women.

Yoga means different things to different people and, reflecting its diversity, there are many types of yoga. Our survey found that it is males and younger people who are more attracted to some of the physically more demanding styles of yoga that have gained in popularity in the West over the past two decades, whereas older age groups went for more relaxing styles. Apart from providing exercise, yoga can also be a form of therapy, meditation or a spiritual path.

Government agencies have found that around 2% of the adult population practise yoga to a greater or lesser extent, with a much lower participation rate for people who have not yet turned 18. Both their research and our survey found that the age group with the highest participation rate in yoga classes is the 35- to 44-year-old group. There has been a slight decline recently in the popularity of yoga; however, this was in the context of a reduction in physical activities overall among the Australian population. A major reason for this trend is not the rise in the popularity of junk food but because more and more people are playing computer games.

56% of the yoga students who responded to our survey attend class once or twice a week. In contrast, and not surprisingly, the same percentage of the yoga teachers in our survey said they taught or practised yoga between five and seven times per week. Most people initially take up yoga to improve their health and fitness – with an emphasis on flexibility and strength – but also in order to reduce stress or as a treatment for a physical problem, particularly for a bad back. Many of the respondents to our survey stated that their reasons for doing yoga changed after they started doing regular practice, with more than half claiming that they keep at it for their personal development, which could be interpreted in a variety of ways.

Although overall yoga promotes physical and mental health, it can cause damage if not done properly, and care needs to be taken with inverted postures such as the headstand and shoulder stand, as well as with the lotus position, which is the cross-legged position

that is commonly associated with yoga and meditation. A common admission in the survey among those who had sustained injuries was that they had pushed themselves too hard. Far less frequently teachers were said to have caused injuries by pushing students too hard.

A large number of our survey respondents reported that they work in health care occupations, and for most of the yoga teachers, teaching yoga is not their only source of income. Among the students the most common health care occupation is nursing, whereas among teachers the largest group worked as massage therapists. Many also worked as nurses, psychologists and practitioners of alternative medicine.

In the survey we also looked at incomes. We didn't ask for individual incomes, but household incomes; that is, the total income of all the people that survey respondents lived with. We found that around three-quarters of the students and 60% of the teachers have a household income above $50,000 per year. Whereas just 9% of the students are on an annual household income below $30,000, one in five of the teachers belong to this group. It would seem that being a yoga teacher is not a path to riches. Yoga itself isn't that expensive, with the average person spending just under $100 a month on yoga practice and accessories.

Overall, yoga was found to have a positive impact on people's lives, with a clear majority concluding that their physical, mental and emotional health, as well as their relationships, were better or much better than before they started doing yoga.

That is the end of Section 4. You now have half a minute to check your answers.

That is the end of the Listening Test. You now have ten minutes to transfer your answers to the answer sheet.

Listening Test 3

You will hear four different recordings and you will have to answer questions on what you hear.

There will be time for you to read the instructions and questions before the recording is played.

You will also have the opportunity to check your answers.

The recordings will be played ONCE only.

The test is in four sections. Write your answers on the question sheet as you listen. At the end of Section 4, you have ten minutes to transfer your answers onto the answer sheet, which is on page 31. When you finish, check the answers at the back of the book.

Now turn to Section 1.

Section 1

You will hear a man having an interview for a job in a hotel. First, you have some time to look at questions 1 to 4.

Now listen and answer questions 1 to 4.

Woman: Good morning, Mr Peters, please come in and have a seat.

Man: Thank you.

Woman: My name's Gloria McKell, I'm the personnel manager here. Now, before we start the job interview, I just need to get a couple of details from you.

Man: Sure.

Woman: Now, first of all I'd just like to confirm I have the correct details. Your name is George Peters, isn't it?

Man: Yes.

Woman: And your contact phone number is 0438 637 935?

Man: That's right.

The man's phone number is 0438 637 935, so '0438 637 935' has been written next to the example on the question paper. Now continue with questions 1 to 4.

Woman: We have vacancies for a couple of positions in our hotel at the moment. Uh, which position are you interested in applying for?

Man: Uh, <u>room service</u>.

Woman: Room service, right. Now I'd like to find out a little about your employment background. Have you worked in a hotel before, or have you been employed in any capacity in the hospitality industry?

Man: I've never actually worked in a hotel, but <u>I've been a waiter</u> in a couple of different places.

Woman: Oh, good. I'm sure that experience will come in handy.

Man: Also, at the moment I'm doing a course.

Woman: Oh, what are you doing?

Man: I'm studying <u>Tourism Management</u>. I'm in the second year of a three-year course.

Woman: That's good to hear. Oh, by the way, we have quite a few international guests staying here. Do you speak any foreign languages?

Man: I did <u>French</u> at high school, and I'm studying <u>Korean</u> as part of my diploma course.

Woman: And how well do you speak those languages?

Man: Well, I can have a simple conversation in French, but my Korean's still fairly basic, though I think it'd come in handy with room service.

Woman: Good.

Before you hear the rest of the conversation, you have some time to look at questions 5 to 10.

Now listen and answer questions 5 to 10.

Woman: Well, I've asked you a number of questions, now I wonder if there's anything you'd like to know about the position or about the hotel.

Man: Um, could you tell me what the duties are of doing room service? I mean, I've got a vague idea, but it'd be good to know exactly what it involves.

Woman: Yes, of course. In fact, your duties would not be limited to room service; there are a few extra things that are now part of the job you're applying for. For instance, the porter used to <u>carry guests' bags to their rooms,</u> but his position has been abolished and that would now be your responsibility. Unlike a waiter, you don't take their orders for food – the kitchen staff does that by phone.

Man: Right.

Woman: If you're on afternoon shift, you also have to take the afternoon newspapers to the guests who've ordered them, but if you're on the morning shift it's done by the concierge. You're qualified to serve alcohol, aren't you?

Man: Yes.

Woman: Good, because on evening shifts you may have to <u>serve in the hotel bar.</u> What else? If a guest calls to say there's a problem with some of the equipment in the room, if it's something simple like one of the light bulbs has blown, then you replace it, but if it's something more complex, say, if the TV isn't working, you leave that to the technical staff.

Man: I see.

Woman: Oh no, sorry, there's been a change in that. In fact, now all electrical work has to be done by the technical staff – it's an occupational health and safety issue.

Man: Better to be safe than sorry, I suppose.

Woman: Yes. You don't have to do any of the cleaning, though you do have to <u>remove any dirty plates the guests have used in their rooms.</u> The cleaners are the ones who make sure the fridges have the right amount of drinks and snacks in them. There are a few other duties, but basically room service plays an important role in maintaining guest satisfaction, and so a friendly attitude and efficiency are what's required.

Man: Oh, that goes without saying. And could I ask about the pay and conditions?

Woman: Of course. The pay's $20 per hour, and $25 per hour between 10 pm and 6 am as well as on Sundays.

Man: Right. And what's provided by the hotel? For instance, I suppose there's a uniform to wear?

Woman: Yes, <u>the hotel provides the jacket and trousers.</u> However, you'd be responsible for doing your own laundry.

Man: Uh-huh. Oh yeah, um, what about transport? Like, if we finish a shift around midnight, does the hotel pay for taxi fares to get back home?

Woman: We used to do that, but now instead <u>we allow staff to park for free</u> on the premises. It can be very hard finding a parking space on the street around this area.

Man: Yeah, I had trouble getting a spot when I came here today.

Woman: Yes, it's a busy area. I might just add that we pride ourselves on having a well-trained staff, so it's a good thing that you're doing your diploma.

Man: Yes, it's been a very interesting course so far.

Woman: Good. Oh, one other thing, <u>we also pay for medical insurance</u> for all our employees as an extra incentive for working with us.

Man: Oh, that's good.

Woman: And until recently we provided one meal per shift as well, but that's been discontinued. Right, well I think that's all then. I'll give you a call later in the week and we can talk further.

Man: Uh-huh. Well, thank you very much.

That is the end of Section 1. You now have half a minute to check your answers.

Now turn to Section 2.

Section 2

Timothy Curtin is an officer at the Department of Immigration. You will hear him talking to foreign students at a business college regarding visa regulations. First, you have some time to look at questions 11 and 12.

Now listen and answer questions 11 to 12.

Good morning, everyone. My name's Timothy Curtin, and I work for the Department of Immigration. I've come along today to give you some information about visa regulations so as to make your stay here a bit easier. I'll be telling you about some of the rules for those on student visas and particularly about how to extend your visa.

Now, I'm from the Atwood office of the Department of Immigration. At our office we mainly <u>process work visas</u>. However, in the office where I used to work, I dealt mainly with student visas, which is why I was chosen to speak to you today. For other matters such as residency applications or medical visas, you need to go to the Hampstead office of the department. For <u>visas for people who are here on holidays</u> you can go to any office of the Department of Immigration.

As you would know, there are certain conditions for people who hold student visas. For instance, if you move, you have to tell your college. The college then has to inform the department by mail, giving both your old and new address. You can change the college where you study, but <u>you have to let the department know that you've enrolled with a new college</u>. You're also allowed to work, but remember that the maximum you can work is 15 hours per week because you're here as full-time students, so your main focus has to be on studies. You can also take up to three weeks' holidays between courses. <u>If your marital status changes, you have to inform the department</u> and provide us with a copy of the marriage certificate within a month of the wedding.

Before you hear the rest of the talk, you have some time to look at questions 13 to 20.

Now listen and answer questions 13 to 20.

What I'd like to do now is to go through the steps you have to follow when you want to extend your student visa, because a lot of students have to do that at some point while they're in this country.

The first thing you have to do if you want to extend your visa is to pay for the next course you're planning to take. As you know, all courses have to be paid in advance. The course itself has to be of at least <u>four months' duration</u> and you are advised to submit your visa application at least two months before the course is due to commence, if possible. You need to keep a copy of the receipt of payment and send us the original. We advise that with all the documents you send us that you keep photocopies for yourself just in case any go missing. You'll also have to get a letter from the college you've been attending, which states your attendance record at that college. You already know that one of the requirements of a student visa is that you turn up to a minimum of 75% of your classes. If you've been absent from more than 25% of classes, you'll have to provide medical certificates stating that you were ill and unable to attend classes on those days.

You then need to fill in a form to extend your student visa. That's Form 726C. You can obtain one by visiting any branch of our department, or else you can access it on the Internet. At the end of my talk I'll be handing out a brochure that gives our website address as well as the addresses of department offices throughout the country. On top of that, you'll also need to be able to show that you have the means to support yourself while in this country. It's been estimated that the average student needs $15,000 a year to live on, and for that reason you will need to prove that you've got at least $6,000 in a bank account. It's got to be a bank account in this country, so $10,000 in a foreign account is of no use. Of course, your passport has to be still valid. And what else? Ah yes, then you'll need three passport photos. Make sure they're fairly recent photos. You then take all these documents and the form down to the Immigration office, along with your passport. As you can see, there's quite a lot to do, so don't leave it till the last minute.

You've got to lodge your application, along with all the documents, at least three weeks before the old visa expires. You have to pay for the visa application too, and that money's non-refundable. You can pay by cash, credit card or cheque. Oh, by the way, it'll cost you $325 to apply for an extension of your student visa. Wait, let me check that. Oh, that's right, it's gone up to $435. Then, it'll take about a week to process your application, but we also have to make allowances for weekends and public holidays, and at times we have heavy workloads, so it may take as long as 12 working days before you get a reply. You might hear from us before that, but don't contact us before that period of time has passed. There may be a few things we need to ask you about before granting a visa, so there's a chance you'll be invited to an interview just so that we can check up on anything. But we'll let you know if we think that's necessary.

Don't worry if you can't remember all these things I've been talking about, they're all on Form 726C. Well, I think that's about enough from me. Now, do any of you have any questions?

That is the end of Section 2. You now have half a minute to check your answers.

Now turn to Section 3.

Section 3

You will hear two marketing students, Maggie and Mike, talking to their teacher about a seminar presentation that they are preparing. First, you have some time to look at questions 21 to 24.

Now listen and answer questions 21 to 24.

Teacher: So, you two are going to give a presentation next week about the beauty industry, aren't you?

Mike: Yeah, we've divided it into two sections. First we'll be looking at the place of the beauty industry in the economy.

Maggie: Yeah, and then we were going to look at what drives it, as well as some recent trends.

Teacher: That sounds like a good way of doing it. OK, Mike, how are you going to be starting off?

Mike: Well, first we were amazed at the size of the industry. It's measured in billions, not millions. It's worth $160 billion a year globally.

Maggie: That figure includes products for haircare – they're worth $38 billion alone. Then there's make-up and perfume – I think that's $15 billion – plus cosmetic surgery, skincare products, diet pills and health clubs.

Mike: In America, more money is spent on beauty than on education.

Teacher: Really?

Maggie: Yeah. The profits of the leading company in the industry have been growing by 14% a year for the last 13 years. And the industry as a whole has been growing at the rate of 7% a year. In India, sales of anti-ageing creams are growing by 40% a year. And you know the Avon ladies? Well, there are 900,000 of them in Brazil, which is more than the number of people in its navy and army.

Teacher: Amazing. Now, just going back a bit, you mentioned cosmetic surgery. Do you have any data on that?

Mike: Yeah. It's worth $20 billion a year now, and the number of procedures they do in the US has jumped by more than 220% since 1997. Botox injections to remove wrinkles are the main thing done these days, but nose jobs and fat removal are still very common. And there's been a real boom in teeth whitening. Also, because the cost of cosmetic surgery has really come down, a lot more people can afford it now.

Teacher: And do you know much about the history of the industry?

Maggie: Well, the modern beauty industry really started up about a hundred years ago. When photography became widespread, it became much easier for the public to see idealised standards of beauty, and people wanted to buy the products to make themselves look like the models they saw in magazines. By the middle of the century, scientific advances led to changes in the ingredients used in many cosmetics, which made them more affordable, and packaging made them more attractive.

Before you hear the rest of the conversation, you have some time to look at questions 25 to 30.

Now listen and answer questions 25 to 30.

Teacher: Now, in the second part of your presentation you're going to be looking at why people buy the products.

Maggie: Yes, that's right. This area is a bit more subjective, and Mike and I disagreed on a few matters.

Mike: Well, marketing is a hit-and-miss affair and it's true what they say, that only half of any marketing budget achieves the desired result.

Maggie: I think that's an exaggeration, don't you? Anyway, there are powerful forces at work in the beauty industry, because when it comes down to it, there's no avoiding the fact that it's all about image and that this industry is so successful because it preys on people's hopes and fears.

Mike: That's a bit harsh, isn't it? It's only natural to try to look your best.

Maggie: Well, the guy who founded Revlon called the whole business 'hope in a jar'.

Teacher: Did he? That's a nice way of putting it.

Mike: We found a British study of 11,000 people which concluded that <u>people who are less attractive earn less money</u>.

Maggie: And that was the case no matter whether they worked as secretaries, in sales or as executives.

Teacher: And why do you think that's the case?

Maggie: Well, I reckon one reason is because <u>attractive people have higher expectations and are less willing to put up with being treated badly</u>.

Mike: Yeah, but there are plenty of good-looking people with low self-esteem who *do* let others walk all over them. I think what it comes down to is that people in general treat good-looking people well. And it starts young. Even three-month-old babies smile longer at faces that adults find attractive.

Teacher: So who judges what's beautiful and what isn't?

Maggie: We didn't really go into that, but it seems that perceptions of beauty are connected to health and fertility. In some places people go for shiny hair, in other cultures women use mascara to make their eyes look bigger and to give themselves a younger look, but a <u>universal indicator of being young and healthy is to have clear skin</u>.

Mike: And that's why so much money is made from skin cleansers, moisturisers, facial creams and so on.

Teacher: Well, there are certainly plenty of tricks to this trade.

Maggie: Yeah, and most of them aren't new tricks at all. I think I could make a link at this part of the presentation to what

Mike was saying about the early 20th century, because there's a trend now in the beauty industry to go back to the approach they had a century ago, when they stressed a connection between beauty and health. They got women to have facials and do exercise classes. Now they aim at beauty, but also <u>like people to be fit</u>, not just thin.

Mike: Oh, come on! The industry just scares people into going on diets that can actually harm them. And most of those thin models aren't in good physical condition, they're just hungry.

Maggie: You can't tell just by looking. Anyway, I'm not denying that image is important. In fact, beauty firms spend up to 25% of their turnover on advertising.

Teacher: That's incredible!

Maggie: Isn't it! And they put just 2 or 3% into research and development. By comparison, in the pharmaceutical industry, 15% of sales goes into research and development.

Teacher: Well, it sounds like you have got the topic well covered. I'm sure the class will really enjoy your presentation.

That is the end of Section 3. You now have half a minute to check your answers.

Now turn to Section 4.

Section 4

You will hear a talk by an archaeological scientist on her latest research. First, you have some time to look at questions 31 to 40.

Now listen and answer questions 31 to 40.

Good morning, ladies and gentlemen. Many of you may remember that in 1991 a couple who were hiking high in the mountains on the border between Italy and Austria found the body of a man who had died 5,300 years ago.

This corpse was later given the nickname 'the Iceman'. Fortunately, a complete set of clothes and a variety of gear were found on or near the corpse, and these give us further clues as to his identity. Today I'd like to speak to you about some of the latest findings on the Iceman.

Scientists have learned from the Iceman's corpse in the same way as detectives investigating a murder gather clues from the victim's body. The study of the Iceman's bones shows that he was 46 years old at the time of death, which is relatively old for people at that time. It appears that he belonged to a group from central northern Europe rather than to the group of people who lived not far to the south of the spot where his body was found. Yet it seems he may have moved around somewhat during his life. Although exactly where he spent his life is unknown, investigation of his tooth enamel suggests that he grew up in one place and then spent several decades in another area.

Samples taken from his stomach and intestines give us an indication of what he'd eaten shortly before his death, including grains, though this does not allow conclusions to be drawn as to what he usually ate. However, samples of his hair show that his usual diet consisted of plants and the meat of several animals. Living in a time long before the development of modern medicine, the tattoos on his back may indicate acupuncture points, yet on the other hand they could simply be a form of body decoration. It seems that he was not in a good state of health in the last six months of his life. There are three lines known as Beau's lines on the single fingernail that was found. These lines occur if the nail stops growing due to illness and then starts growing again.

It was initially assumed that he had died of the cold in autumn because of the presence of a piece of fruit that ripens in late summer. Yet there is now strong botanical evidence that he died in spring. This is because pollen of the hop hornbeam tree was found in his intestines, and that small tree blooms only in late spring. So he may have breathed some in or drunk some water containing the pollen shortly before his death.

So, what else do we know about the Iceman? He ate a primitive form of wheat, which was baked into bread on an open fire. Although leaves of moss were found in his intestines, it appears that moss was not part of his diet but had probably entered his mouth by accident. In those days the local people had no paper bags or plastic wrapping, and so used moss to pack food in. Moss was a very versatile plant, with different varieties that grew far to the north being used by the Vikings as toilet paper.

The equipment found around the body gives us many clues as to his way of life. He was well prepared for climbing through the mountains: he had a jacket made from deer hide and goat hide, and a pair of shoes made from the skin of both goat and bear and then insulated with plant material. Over the top of it all he was wearing a cape made from grass and bast, which is made from bark. This could give us a clue as to his occupation. In fact, this cape resembles capes still worn by shepherds in the Balkans, and the site where he was found is near an area where shepherds traditionally take their flocks in summer. Yet the theory that he was a shepherd has little else to support it. It's been proposed that he was a hunter due to the fact that he was carrying a bow and some arrows. Some earlier ideas that he was a warrior or a trader of flint have been abandoned for lack of any supporting material.

The Iceman was found lying on a large rock, and so it was believed initially that he had fallen asleep on the rock and then died. However, the consensus now is that he died nearby and then floated into that position during periods when the ice thawed. There are several indicators for this: first, the awkward position of his left arm; second, the position of his right hand, which was stuck under another rock; third, the missing outer layer of skin; and the fact that some of his belongings were a few metres from the body.

Despite these interesting findings, there are still many things that we don't know about the Iceman. What was he doing up there high in the mountains, apparently by himself? Did he die from exhaustion and cold while running away from danger? We may never know exactly what the cause of death was, because this would require an autopsy, which has not been allowed as it would cause too much damage to the corpse. When the body was first removed, it was thought to be that of a missing mountain climber, and a number of people disturbed the site, wrecking a good part of the evidence in the process. But, hopefully, with further research we will be able to solve some of the mysteries that still surround the Iceman, who has already taught us so much about the way of life at that time.

That is the end of Section 4. You now have half a minute to check your answers.

That is the end of the Listening Test. You now have ten minutes to transfer your answers to the answer sheet.

Listening Test 4

You will hear four different recordings and you will have to answer questions on what you hear.

There will be time for you to read the instructions and questions before the recording is played.

You will also have the opportunity to check your answers.

The recordings will be played ONCE only.

The test is in four sections. Write your answers on the question sheet as you listen. At the end of Section 4, you have ten minutes to transfer your answers onto the answer sheet, which is on page 31. When you finish, check the answers at the back of the book.

Now turn to Section 1.

Section 1

A woman has just arrived at a shopping mall with her children. You will hear her talking to a man at the information desk. First, you have some time to look at questions 1 to 6 and the floor plan of the shopping mall.

Now listen and answer questions 1 to 6.

Man: Good morning, can I help you?

Woman: Yes. I've never been here before and I've just got a few questions about where a few places are here.

Man: Fine. Here's a floor plan of the mall, you can take that with you, but if you have any questions, I'd be very happy to help.

Woman: Well, I'm afraid I always find these floor plans a bit confusing, so could you just show me exactly where we are on this?

Man: No problem. Here we are at the information desk, right in the middle, next to the escalators.

The man says they are at the information desk and that it is in the middle, next to the escalator. Therefore, 'C' has been written next to the example on the question paper. Now continue with questions 1 to 6.

Woman: Right. Now, I heard there's a children's play centre where you can leave your children while you do the shopping.

Man: That's right. You can see it on the floor plan; it's in the corner, to the left of the supermarket. There are plenty of toys for them to play with there – also, there's fresh fruit to eat and they can have fun with the other children.

Woman: Sounds good, doesn't it, kids? I was thinking I might take them to have their hair cut first. Is that the hairdresser between the furniture shop and the children's clothes shop?

Man: Yes, it is. They do children's haircuts as well.

Woman: Oh, lovely. Now, my little boy's going to a friend's birthday party next week, and we wanted to buy a present. Do you know if there are any stores that might have things a seven-year-old boy would like?

Man: Oh yes, there's a toy store right next to the shoe shop. They've got a good range of toys. I'm sure you'll find something for a child of that age. I often buy things there myself. The prices are quite reasonable.

Woman: Oh, that's good to hear. Oh, and also, are there any toilets on this floor?

Man: Yes, they're in a bit of a hidden corner. You just go past the bookstore – you can see they sell newspapers there too – and down the corridor.

Woman: Ah, yes, I see. I'd better take them there before we go to the hairdresser. What else do I need to do? Oh yeah, I've got to buy some credit for my mobile phone. Can I do that at the phone kiosk over there near those benches?

Man: Yes, you can. You can also do it at the supermarket if you want.

Woman: Right. Now, we've just come up from the car park, but we took the escalator. I might have a lot of things to carry later on, so I was wondering if there's an elevator.

Man: Yes, it's next to the computer store, near the top of the stairs.

Woman: Oh yes, I can see it now.

Before you hear the rest of the conversation, you have some time to look at questions 7 to 10.

Now listen and answer questions 7 to 10.

Woman: Oh, when I parked the car I couldn't see how much you have to pay for parking.

Man: It's free for the first two hours, but after that it's $3 an hour.

Woman: Hmm. I think with all the things we have to do, we might be here for more than two hours. So if you park there for three hours altogether, you have to pay $3, and if it's four hours, you pay $6 and so on.

Man: Yes, that's right.

Woman: Uh-huh. How about the children's play centre. Is there any charge for leaving your children there?

Man: Oh no, that's a free service of the shopping mall. However, there's a policy that the children have to be at least 18 months old.

Woman: My youngest is just 10 months old, but I'd rather keep her with me anyway. Also, we might need to get something to eat later. Is there any place to buy lunch?

Man: Oh yes, you can get all kinds of things at the food court, from snacks to fast food to healthy meals. There's a really good range. It's two floors up on level five. It's best to take the elevator.

Woman: Do you know if they have pizza? Both my kids really love pizza.

Man: Yes, they do. Oh, did you know you can watch a movie here, too?

Woman: Yes, I've heard <u>there's a cinema on the top floor</u>. There might be something on that my kids'd be interested in.

Man: Yeah, there are a couple of children's films on at the moment.

Woman: Well, thank you very much; you've been a great help.

Man: My pleasure.

That is the end of Section 1. You now have half a minute to check your answers.

Now turn to Section 2.

Section 2

You will hear a talk by a representative of an agency that finds people to look after homes when their owners are away. He is talking to a group of homeowners. First, you have some time to look at questions 11 to 20.

Now listen and answer questions 11 to 20.

Good evening, ladies and gentlemen, I'm glad you've been able to make it to this introductory talk about our agency, which is called Contented Homes. My name's Gary and I'm going to explain what our business involves, but first I'd like to tell you something about the background of our agency.

We commenced operations <u>back in 1989</u>, and essentially our job is to find suitable people to live in and look after other people's homes while they're away. The homeowners – people like yourselves – might be away on holidays or temporarily working in another city or country, and they want to be sure that while they're away, their home will be secure, and that when they come back, everything will be in good condition. When we first started out, we conducted most of our business over the phone, but now the bulk of it is done <u>over the Internet</u>.

Basically, this is how it works: homeowners come to us when they need to find reliable, trustworthy people to take good care of their home for a limited period of time. The people who stay in your home and take care of it are called 'housesitters'. The housesitters live at your place for periods of anything between <u>one month</u> and two years.

There are all kinds of reasons why people housesit. Some are couples, others are single. Often they're saving up to buy their own home, or they may be renovating their own home and just need somewhere to stay temporarily, or they might have just moved to your city. Although <u>housesitters don't pay you any rent</u> when they're living in your home, they are required to pay any bills for the telephone, gas, electricity and so on. So, for the homeowner, this is not a way to make money.

When someone registers with us to become a housesitter, they provide us with some of their personal details such as their age and occupation. I need to stress here that our agency *does not* carry out a security check on the people who have registered with us to be housesitters. Many housesitters have references from people whose houses or apartments they've looked after in the past. <u>It's up to you to check those references</u>. Allowing someone to live in your home is not a decision to be taken lightly, so we also recommend that you meet with any prospective housesitters and interview them before deciding which person or people would be most suitable to look after your home in your absence.

There are similarities between housesitters and tenants, but there are differences as well. <u>Housesitters don't have as many rights</u> as people who have a lease on a property. As the homeowner, you can give a spare set of keys to your home to a neighbour, friend or relative. That person's allowed to drop in on the housesitters without prior notice at any time – within reason – to check that the house is in order, and the housesitters aren't allowed to stop them from entering.

There are many good reasons to use the services of a housesitter. Burglars soon notice when people are away, so theft is much less likely if someone is living in your home. But it's not simply a matter of security. Housesitters keep your home clean and tidy. Some of them are even more houseproud than the actual owners. In addition, many people need a housesitter to look after pets and keep the garden in order.

Now I'd like tell you about the fees we charge. First, *you* the homeowners don't have to pay us anything. When people who want to be housesitters come to us, they have to pay $375 to go into our directory. That's where we get the money to run our service. As I said, we don't check to see that the information supplied by them is correct; it would simply cost us far too much time and money to do that.

When you've decided that you want to go ahead and have a housesitter look after your home, we definitely think it's a good idea for you to take out insurance for your home. You'll find that many insurance companies prefer the higher degree of security if someone's living in your home than if it's left empty. Anyway, I hope I've given you a clear idea of our service, and now I'd be happy to take any questions.

That is the end of Section 2. You now have half a minute to check your answers.

Now turn to Section 3.

Section 3

You will hear two students talking to their teacher about a seminar paper they are preparing for their Population Studies class.

First, you have some time to look at questions 21 to 25.

Now listen and answer questions 21 to 25.

Teacher: So, how's your seminar paper going?

Woman: Oh, it's almost ready. My head's just full of statistics at the moment.

Teacher: Is there anything you found particularly interesting?

Man: Yeah, for instance, about where people choose to live when they migrate to Australia. The focus of our talk is on migration to Sydney, but we found we needed to look briefly at migration to other parts of Australia as well.

Woman: Hmm. Most migrants go to the big cities, but it isn't the same for all nationalities. For instance, over the last five years, with the British, only about one third of them altogether went to Sydney and Melbourne.

Teacher: So, where did most of them go?

Man: Oh, all over the place, but for some reason quite a few ended up over in Perth.

Teacher: That's not a bad place to live.

Man: No. But with the Chinese, 26% of them choose to live in Melbourne and 58% in Sydney.

Teacher: Really? Do you have any idea why the Chinese and British have such different settlement patterns?

Man: Well, not really. Sometimes it's hard to find out exactly why people choose to live where they do. There's a thriving Lebanese community in Melbourne, but more than seven out of ten people from Lebanon were drawn to Sydney.

Teacher: I see. So you've covered groups from Europe, East Asia and the Middle East. Do you have anything on people from other regions?

Woman: Yes. When we went through data from the Department of Immigration and the Bureau of Statistics, we found that in the case of the Malaysians, for some reason only a minority chose Sydney and Melbourne, but I don't know exactly where most of them ended up. I think quite a few of them were attracted to Queensland because of the climate.

Teacher: Yeah, it must be hard for people coming from a tropical region to get used to colder winters. What about the New Zealanders?

Man: Well, they don't need a visa for Australia, so they're counted separately from all other nationalities, but the vast bulk of them have ended up in Sydney. You'd think that Melbourne'd be more to their liking because its climate's more like what they're used to and the distance from New Zealand to Melbourne is about the same.

Before you hear the rest of the conversation, you have some time to look at questions 26 to 30.

Now listen and answer questions 26 to 30.

Teacher: You also looked into *why* people choose the places they do, didn't you?

Woman: Yes. Well, people often go where the work is. I mean, it's no use finding a nice place to live if you're going to be unemployed. But there's a more decisive factor, and that is that people generally like to live near their friends and relatives, and with people from their own country, so they won't be so isolated. And they do that despite the higher housing prices in the larger cities.

Teacher: Yeah, rents are getting ridiculous. But hasn't Sydney always attracted people – I mean, even people born elsewhere in Australia?

Woman: Well, historically that was the case, but even though Sydney's grown a lot recently, there's been hardly any increase in the number of Australian-born people living in Sydney.

Teacher: Why is that? I mean, I can understand why people would be leaving; a lot of people feel Sydney's getting too crowded and hectic.

Woman: But that can't be the reason because they often end up in places such as south-east Queensland, where the infrastructure simply isn't coping with the rapid population growth and faster pace of life.

Man: The research shows that the ones leaving Sydney are particularly middle-aged and elderly people who own the place they live in. By selling their Sydney home when they retire and buying and living in a cheaper one elsewhere, they then have more funds left over.

Teacher: It must be difficult making that shift at their age.

Woman: I think moving or migrating's hard for *anyone*.

Teacher: Quite right. But what effect is migration having?

Woman: Well, there are all kinds of effects, but sociologists talk about a growing gap between Sydney and Melbourne on the one hand, and the rest of the country on the other. You see, the most recent data shows that 60% of the overseas arrivals went to those two cities, even though Sydney and Melbourne combined have got just 40% of the country's population.

Teacher: But you've got to remember that Australia is one of the most urbanised countries in the world. A good 50% of the population live in the state capitals, not including the urban fringes. Is anything being done to promote growth in other regions?

Man: Well, the government's got several proposals. We need more people in rural areas, but no one's suggesting that we encourage farmers to migrate to Australia because agriculture's very capital-intensive in this country. But the government's thinking about having lower tax rates on private firms that employ newly arrived migrants in towns outside Sydney and Melbourne. Of course, these days the government doesn't want to actually provide jobs for them but they are willing to favour employers who employ them.

Teacher: Do you think that'd work?

Woman: I don't know. There's nothing to stop them moving to one of the two big cities if they feel like it.

Teacher: Exactly.

Woman: In fact, the statistics don't give the full picture. When they migrate, people very often initially live outside of Sydney, so in the statistics they're recorded as having settled outside Sydney. But then after a while many make the move to Sydney. So the real picture's even more out of balance than what the statistics say.

Teacher: Statistics really can be a slippery thing sometimes, can't they?

Woman: That's for sure.

That is the end of Section 3. You now have half a minute to check your answers.

Now turn to Section 4.

Section 4

Emma Bell is an agricultural scientist. In the following lecture she describes some of the advantages of the hemp plant. First, you have some time to look at questions 31 to 40.

Now listen and answer questions 31 to 40.

When we think of progress, we tend to look to the future. However, the past can also provide inspiration. Today I'd like to outline some of the many ways in which the hemp plant – a plant that was used very widely until the early 20th century – can benefit both humans and the environment.

You may remember that when the use of computers became more widespread, there was much talk of the 'paperless office', yet now far more paper is being used than ever before. Most of that paper is made from wood, but it can also be made from hemp. Hemp is a fast-growing annual plant that can be harvested within four months of germination, whereas a tree takes 20 years. This means that a hectare of hemp can produce 80 times as much paper as a hectare of trees. In fact, hemp was the main source for paper production until the 20th century and the paper it makes is of superior quality to that made from wood. Many of the rivers in the vicinity of today's paper mills suffer the effects of pollution from bleach and other chemicals used in the manufacture of paper from wood. In contrast, paper made from hemp does not require bleach.

So much clothing these days is made from cotton. Yet fabric has been made from hemp for over 7,000 years. The trouble with cotton crops is that they take a heavy toll on the environment and are often dependent on irrigation. Hemp can grow using far less water and does not need as much fertiliser or pesticides. In fact, hemp crops even have a natural resistance to pests. Clothes made from the tough fibre of hemp also last longer than those made from cotton, which is not something that'll make clothing manufacturers very happy. But another way in which hemp is the superior material is that it's more effective in blocking out UV rays from the sun, which can cause skin cancer. To top it off, clothing made from hemp is very comfortable to wear.

In parts of the world that still don't have electricity, this versatile plant can also be used to light lamps. Back in the days of sailing ships, when hemp was used to make ropes and sails, lamps were often fuelled by <u>whale oil</u>, which gave off a much stronger-smelling black smoke. The pursuit of that oil was one of the reasons for the existence of the whaling industry, which hunted many species of whale almost to extinction.

Closer to our own time, Henry Ford used hemp in the production of his first cars. These days, with panels being made of metal, even a minor accident can lead to costly repairs. Being derived from a plant, <u>hemp panels would be less expensive</u>. Yet perhaps an even more significant consequence would be that, instead of old cars being left to rust by the roadside, an abandoned car made from hemp would rot faster. A further advantage in the case of automobiles is the fuel. One of the major causes of global warming is the use of fossil fuels in cars and trucks. Methanol is an alternative to petrol, and it can be extracted from hemp. This fuel is already used by racing cars, and it <u>doesn't produce as much air pollution</u>, thus placing a smaller burden on the air we breathe.

Hemp is also a source for a variety of foods. The oil that is obtained from the plant can be used to make cooking oil, butter, cheese and even ice-cream. <u>Flour</u> derived from hemp has a greater protein content than normal wheat flour, and its seeds contain all the amino acids, providing a form of protein that's more easily digested than that in soybeans.

Carpets made from hemp are more durable than other carpets and are resistant to mildew, which grows in humid or damp conditions. It can also be used in the home to produce furnishings such as fibreboard, furniture and even plastics. Paints and varnish made from petrochemicals <u>contain poisons, whereas this is not the case with those produced from hemp</u>.

Hemp plants are best grown close together, and because they produce an abundance of leaves, the ground underneath the plants is shaded, which hinders the growth of weeds, so farmers don't have to spend money on potentially dangerous herbicides. It thrives in areas with <u>low rainfall</u> and may be useful in combating salinity because it doesn't need irrigation and its long taproot can reach underground nutrients and water.

As a fast-growing plant, it's an easily renewable, biodegradable and ecologically sustainable source of a vast range of products that are currently made from polluting resources such as coal, metals, gas and oil. This is quite plainly a case where we can make progress by learning from the past.

That is the end of Section 4. You now have half a minute to check your answers.

That is the end of the Listening Test. You now have ten minutes to transfer your answers to the answer sheet.

Answer key

LISTENING

Listening Test 1

SECTION 1

1 Penny Ryan
2 24 March 1982 // March 24(,) 1982 // 24.(0)3.(19)82 // (0)3.24.(19)82
3 Blacktown // Black Town
4 7690 3275
5 monthly // every month // once a month
6 A   7 C   8 B
9 B   10 A

SECTION 2

11 shoes
12 beach cafe
13 7 (am/a.m.) to/till/until/– 6 (pm/p.m.) // 7 to 6 // 7–6
14 twice a/per week // Tuesday(s) and Friday(s)
15 on (the/your) balcony/balconies
16 birds, fish
17 11 (pm/p.m.) // 11 at night
18 A, E   19 B, D   20 D, E

SECTION 3

21 B   22 A   23 D   24 E
25 F   26 C   27 C   28 B
29 A   30 B

SECTION 4

31 (nomadic) lifestyle // nomadism
32 clothes/clothing
33 milk, meat   34 gardening
35 feed // eat   36 salt
37 C   38 C   39 A   40 B

Listening Test 2

SECTION 1

1 (Class) C/c // C/c licence/license
2 28 River   3 3701 8699
4 student card   5 (by) cash
6 C   7 B   8 B
9 C   10 A

SECTION 2

11 B   12 F   13 C   14 G
15 D   16 D   17 E   18 G
19 A   20 F

SECTION 3

21 B   22 B   23 A   24 B
25 B   26 C   27 D   28 C
29 B   30 H

SECTION 4

31 reason(s) // motivation(s)
32 funding limitations // funds limited// limited funds/funding
33 85%
34 exercise, therapy
35 computer games
36 reduce stress
37 personal development
38 B   39 B   40 A

Listening Test 3

SECTION 1

1 room service
2 waiter
3 Tourism Management
4 French, Korean
5, 6, 7 *In any order:* B, F, G (clear away plates, take luggage to rooms, work in hotel bar)
8, 9, 10 *In any order:* C, D, G (medical insurance, parking, uniforms)

SECTION 2

11 A, E
12 B, D
13 four/4 months/mths
14 75%
15 (on/via/through) the Internet // online
16 $6,000
17 passport photos
18 $435
19 working days
20 interview

SECTION 3

21 C   22 A   23 B   24 C
25 B   26 A   27 C   28 A
29 C   30 A

SECTION 4

31 B   32 H   33 D   34 C
35 E   36 A   37 C   38 B
39 A   40 B

Listening Test 4

SECTION 1

1 A   2 H   3 I   4 G
5 D   6 F
7 $6 // $6.00 // six dollars
8 eighteen/18 months // 1½ years
9 (on) (level/floor) five/5 // (the) fifth/5th (level/floor)
10 (a) cinema/theatre

SECTION 2

11 1989
12 Internet
13 one/1 month
14 rent
15 reference(s)
16 rights
17 theft/thieves // burglary/burglar(s)
18 pet(s), garden(s)
19 $375
20 (home) insurance

SECTION 3

21 C   22 B   23 B   24 C
25 B   26 B   27 C   28 C
29 A   30 A

SECTION 4

31 4/four months
32 bleach
33 water/irrigation
34 skin cancer // UV/ultraviolet rays
35 whale oil // oil from/of whales
36 less expensive // cheaper
37 (air) pollution
38 C   39 E   40 A

READING

Reading Test 1

READING PASSAGE 1

1 FALSE; (*The domestic clock was not exactly invented; it was probably a spin-off from the scientific activities ... the church assistant needed to know when to warn the watchman to ring the bell in the watchtower to warn the local people about some communal activity*)

2 FALSE; (*It was a valuable possession, and when the family moved it went with them*)

3 NOT GIVEN; not stated in the text.

4 TRUE; (*The use of a coiled spring instead of a weight to provide power made possible first the portable clock and subsequently the smaller, personal clock, which was later called a watch.*)

5 TRUE; (*The means adopted to overcome these disadvantages, which directly affected timekeeping accuracy, were twofold.*)

6 iron; (*So possibly it was the watchman's clock on the wall that became the domestic iron clock*)

7 wooden brackets; (*it became fashionable to ... mount these clocks on wooden brackets*)

8 France; (*Spring clocks were first made in France in the 1400s*)

9 (source of) force/power; (*the coiled spring did not provide a constant source of power. When wound up, the spring gave a force that was very strong ... The force then decreased unevenly*)

10 trumpet-shaped (object) // trumpet; (*A fusee is a trumpet-shaped object*)

11 (a) strong thread; (*The trumpet-shaped part has a spiral groove cut in it, and a length of strong thread attached to the groove*)

12 (a) key; (*When the fusee is turned with a key, the thread is pulled off the barrel, which winds up the spring inside it.*)

13 (a) constant speed; (*The thread is wound on the fusee groove, which becomes smaller and smaller in diameter, so that in effect it means that the spring drives the clock at a constant speed.*)

READING PASSAGE 2

14 iv; all three sentences in paragraph A describe what is usually done.

15 iii; (topic sentence: *The truth is that nobody can be sure where an individual piece of rubbish will end up or how the junk in the landfill got there.*)

16 vii; (topic sentence: *New research is planning to find out.*)

17 v; (*The idea is to help plan for an ideal world of waste disposal*)

18 i; (*Part of the problem is that we do not know what we are dealing with ... almost nothing is known about what happens to the waste.*)

19 ix; (*each ... gives a very different set of environmental challenges.*)

20 viii; (*we need to get a clearer picture of the life cycle of different kinds of waste, which is how the tracking project can give useful information.*)

21 x; (*As commodities become scarce in the following centuries, we may have to mine landfills for their riches*)

22 & 23 C/E; (*the mass is measured, but not in terms of the content ... In terms of environmental impact, it is the content, not the number of tonnes, that matters; there is a more fundamental reason to tag trash: to find out where society stores the materials that it mines from the Earth and temporarily turns into products.*)

24 (an) aluminium can; (*An aluminium can, for instance, could have a variety of fates.*)

25 Seattle; (*tracked 60 pieces of trash in Seattle ... The next phase of the experiment will begin – 1,000 more pieces of garbage will be electronically tagged and thrown away in ... Seattle*)

26 green supply chains; (*While a lot of effort has gone into creating green supply chains to bring products to customers*)

27 household waste; (*Within the harmless-sounding category of 'household waste' ... lies everything from carrot peelings to used babies' nappies and low-energy light bulbs ... or old electrical appliances*)

READING PASSAGE 3

28 F; (*primatologists have seen apes hide food from the alpha male or steal his females.*)

29 D; (*they had no opportunity to be taught about tools. Yet soon after they fledged, all picked up sticks to probe busily into cracks*)

30 B; (*"Well, they share our ancestry – of course they're smart." ... our last common ancestor with all birds was a reptile that lived over 300 million years ago.*)

31 A; (*because of their long association with humans*)

32 E; (*Birds can cheat too.*)

33 C; (*Scientists think that dogs were domesticated about 15,000 years ago, a relatively short time in which to develop language skills.*)

34 A; (*the first jay will return to move the nut when the other jay is gone.*)

35 B; (*his research demonstrates that some birds posses what is often another uniquely human skill: the ability to recall a specific past event.*)

36 NO; (*People were surprised to discover that chimpanzees make tools*)

37 YES; (*Something about the environment of both species favored the evolution of tool-making neural powers.*)

38 NOT GIVEN; there is no claim about chimpanzees enjoying problem-solving.

39 NO; (*Even after years of monitoring them in the wild, researchers couldn't determine if the birds' ability was innate, or if they learned to make and use their tools by watching one another.*)

40 YES; (*Such deceptive acts require a complicated form of thinking*)

Reading Test 2

READING PASSAGE 1

1 E; (*some think the crop yield would be too low to make economic sense / the basic premise is flawed.*)

2 A; (*market gardens on the edges of urban areas supplying fresh food straight to your table may soon be over; mass city-centre farming may soon replace them.*)

3 D; (*Indoor crops require less pesticide and are less subject to the problems in nature*)

4 A; (*involving rooftop gardening in Manhattan. While that was interesting, it couldn't be sustained on a mass scale.*)

5 F; (*Despommier has the backing of ... venture capitalists*)

6 C; (*the use of a type of shellfish to filter water. These can clean urban sewage to a state suitable for irrigation.*)

7 8.6 billion; (section B: *The world population is expected to grow by three billion to 8.6 billion over the next half century.*)

8 80 per cent/80%; (section B: *By then, some 80 per cent of the world's population will live in cities*)

9 over one-third; (section B: *with over one-third of the world's surface currently used for agriculture.*)

10 Brazil; (section B: *in the next five decades an area of new arable land roughly the size of Brazil will be required to feed the world's growing population*)

11 solar panels; (section C: *more efficient solar panels for energy* / section D: *solar panels to provide electricity.*)

12 light; (section D: *vertical farming is not without its challenges. One is light – artificial lighting uses a great deal of electricity and generates considerable heat. Another is cost*)

13 within this generation; (section F: *Luc Mougeout ... says the vertical farm is not only possible, but will happen within this generation.*)

READING PASSAGE 2

14 E; (*Newton discovered that mirrors gave an improved image, which allowed a much more accurate view of the heavens. Furthermore, mirrors were easier to manufacture than lenses and could be made larger*)

15 D; (*Copernicus had assumed that the planets moved in a circular path around the Sun, but Kepler found that they did not; they moved in ellipses.*)

16 B; (*He [Copernicus] tried to explain the mathematics behind the planets' movements but found that the circular movement of a sphere could not explain why, for example, Mars apparently stopped and went backwards for a short time.*)

17 B; (*He [Copernicus] discovered that the planets' movements could be far more easily predicted if not the Earth but the Sun were placed in the centre of the system, and the planets circled the Sun rather than the Earth.*)

18 E; (*Yet it was Newton's discovery of the laws of gravity that explained why the planets move the way they do.*)

19 D; (*The German astronomer Johannes Kepler used it to discover that the Copernican observations were not quite correct ... Copernicus had assumed that the planets moved in a circular path around the Sun, but Kepler found that they did not*)

20 fixed stars; (*some of the lights in the sky seemed permanent in relation to each other and these were known as the 'fixed stars'*)

21 (the) planets; (*other lights moved about much more freely and were called 'the wanderers'. We now know the latter as the planets*)

22 (heavenly) music; (*created heavenly music as they moved*)

23 sphere; (*the planets each had a sphere that moved independently of the others*)

24 convex lens; (*Lippershey who used a convex lens*)

25 eyepiece; (*focusing light into an eyepiece*)

26 concave mirror; (*Newton discovered that a concave mirror*)

27 flat secondary mirror; (*reflecting light onto a flat secondary mirror*)

READING PASSAGE 3

28 A; (*Detailed observations are made of the way in which different kinds of people speak in different social situations. The parameters that demonstrate these differences are known as linguistic variables.*)

29 D; (*It is likely that the same gradual process of change affects whole languages as well as dialects.*)

30 D; (*It is easy to recognize a change in language – but only after it has taken place.*)

31 B; (*climatology (which is a consequence of human physical location – the mountain dweller having a physiological different capacity for speech compared with the valley dweller).*)

32 D; (*scientific research, which has shown that there is no single reason for language change.*)

33 C; (*When people move away from each other, their language will diverge.*)

34 A; (*Subconscious change, where people are not aware of the direction in which their speech is moving, is less noticeable, but far more common.*)

35 NO; (*Some speakers introduce the change into their speech before others*)

36 YES; (*a change spreads through a language in much the same way as a stone sends ripples across a pool. But even this implies too regular a movement to account for the reality of sociolinguistic variation.*)

37 NO; (*Historical dictionaries always give an approximate date of entry for a new word or meaning – but these dates invariably reflect the earliest known use of that word in the written language. The first use of the word in speech is always an unknown number of years previous to that.*)

38 NOT GIVEN; the electronic media are not mentioned in the text.

39 YES; (*Some change is the result of one population imperfectly learning the language of another.*)

40 YES; (*The minority language forms a small group that in the long term influences majority usage.*)

Reading Test 3

READING PASSAGE 1

1 E; (*Irrigation would have boosted harvests.*)

2 F; (*The most logical explanation is that a dam failed. The river may have chewed into the dam, gradually weakening it. Perhaps it was washed away by an unusually heavy flood*)

3 A; (*As many as 750,000 people lived in Angkor, its capital, making it the most extensive urban complex of the pre-industrial world.*)

4 C; (*as many as 200,000 Khmer workers may have been needed*)

5 D; (*Today's researchers have been amazed by the ambition of Angkor's early engineers.*)

6 B; (*Exactly what caused the decline is not known; invaders, a change of religion, a shift to maritime trade that condemned an inland city are all guesswork. / Recent excavations ... are suggesting a new answer.*)

7 vi; (paragraph A: *when Portuguese missionaries came across ... Angkor Wat ... the empire was in its final phase.*)

8 iii; (paragraph E: *When other kingdoms in South-East Asia were struggling with too little or too much water, Angkor's waterworks would have been an extremely valuable asset.*)

9 iv; (paragraph C: *To this day the rectangular reservoir is fed by water diverted from the Siem Reap river.*)

10 i; (paragraph E: *during a poor monsoon season, and the ability to divert and hold water would have afforded a measure of protection*)

11 NOT GIVEN; missionaries are referred to in paragraph A, but damage not mentioned in the text.

12 FALSE; (paragraph B: *The people of Angkor left not a single word explaining their kingdom's collapse.*)

13 TRUE; (paragraph D: *Over several centuries, hundreds of miles of canals and dykes ... were constructed*)

14 TRUE; (paragraph F: *generations of Khmer engineers coped with a water system that grew ever more complex and unruly.*)

READING PASSAGE 2

15 wonderland; (*it is a wonderland with flowers of great beauty*)

16 87 per cent; (*this one corner of the continent contains no less than 12,000 different plant species and 87 per cent of them grow nowhere else in the world.*)

17 (a) shallow sea; (*Australia was partly covered by a shallow sea that separated the western part of the continent from the rest.*)

18 sand // desert; (*As Australia gradually warmed, this sea dried up, but it left behind a wide expanse of sand*)

19 B; (*The land here is so poor in nutrients*)

20 C; (*now they are not only well able to survive its destruction but have come to depend on it*)

21 A; (*The eucalypts or gum trees that grow there often take the peculiar form known as mallee ... they have a massive rootstock from which rise half a dozen thin trunks of a common height.*)

22 D; (*But it will not shed any seed they produce unless there is a fire.*)

23 C; (*the intense heat causes the capsules to open. By releasing their seeds only after a fire*)

24 FALSE; (*very few of which have been seen growing in the wild before*)

25 TRUE; (*The eucalypts or gum trees that grow there often take the peculiar form known as mallee. Species that elsewhere become normal-looking trees grow here in such a different way that they might be thought to be a completely different kind.*)

26 NOT GIVEN; not mentioned in the text (The comparison between eucalypts in the south-western area and elsewhere relates only to the mallee.)

27 NOT GIVEN; not mentioned in the text (It is possible to tell how long it has been since there was a fire.)

28 TRUE; (*However, the core of this trunk is not timber but fibre and what seems to be bark, is, in fact, the tightly compacted bases of the leaves*)

READING PASSAGE 3

29 iii; (*Such vast distances would seem to put the stars well beyond the reach of human explorers*)

30 v; (*these ambitious schemes have their disadvantages, and it is doubtful they could really go the distance.*)

31 i; (*there are two radical new possibilities ... that might just enable us ... to reach the stars.*)

32 iv; (*Such observations suggest that dark matter outweighs the universe's visible matter by a factor of about six. So a dark matter starship could pick up its fuel on the way and would therefore not need to carry any.*)

33 ix; (*It is speculated that dark matter particles could be made to collide, thus annihilating each other and converting their mass to energy.*)

34 ii; (*A black hole weighing about a million tonnes would make a perfect energy source*)

35 viii; (*theorists ... prefer an alternative proposal of making one. To create a black hole ...*)

36 & 37 C/D; (*a spacecraft powered by dark matter; a craft powered by an artificial black hole*)

38 particles; (*dark matter particles could be made to collide*)

39 energy; (*converting their mass to energy*)

40 annihiliation; (*The matter could be collected and compressed, which would increase its annihiliation rate*)

Reading Test 4

READING PASSAGE 1

1 C; (*the price of the share will go up until they stop buying. This may have nothing to do with the essential soundness of the company.*)

2 A; (*you are a part-owner, or shareholder, in the company, with the right to share in its profits, to attend board meetings and to vote*)

3 E; (*The advantage to the original owners of selling their shares is that, if the offering is successful, they can realize very large sums of cash.*)

4 C; (*all sorts of factors influence the price of shares*)

5 D; (*This capitalist system of financing big business is fundamental to the world's present economic system.*)

6 (a) high-tech company; Remember that hyphenated words count as one word. (*how, for example, do you value a high-tech company whose products change every few months, and whose real earning power resides in the brains of its talented employees?*)

7 (the) market capitalisation; (*the market capitalization – which is essentially the total value of all a company's shares at the current market price*)

8 (the) casino; (*The soundest, best-established companies are known as 'blue chips'. The term 'blue chip' comes from the world of the casino*)

9 growth stocks; (*'Growth stocks' are shares in newer companies that are expected to do well in the future, but which may not do so.*)

10 tycoons; (*For instance, tycoons may decide they can do a better job of building the business by taking a company private because the red tape and potential for interference by other shareholders is much less.*)

11 TRUE; (*with the right to share in its profits, to attend board meetings and to vote on key issues and appointments.*)

12   NOT GIVEN; the number of shares permitted to a shareholder is not discussed.

13   TRUE; (*one of the main factors is the behaviour of people who buy shares, or, as some would have it, 'the madness of crowds'. If many investors think the price of a share is going to go up and buy it, the price of the share will go up until they stop buying.*)

14   FALSE; (*The rules for going public are quite strict*)

READING PASSAGE 2

15   FALSE; (*The Royal Flying Doctor Service has over the past century provided medical services to those in the outback*)

16   NOT GIVEN; Lieutenant Peel's job is not stated.

17   TRUE; (*On 15 May 1928, the Australian Inland Mission Aerial Medical Service commenced business in Cloncurry, Queensland*)

18   NOT GIVEN; the length of the flights is not mentioned.

19   TRUE; (*It was only in the 1960s that the RFDS had begun purchasing its own aircraft*)

20   E; (*in the 1960s ... RFDS had begun purchasing its own aircraft*)

21   B; (*was employing pilots and engineers directly*)

22   G; (*later models were American in design and manufacture*)

23   A; (*from exposed cockpits to pressurised cabins*)

24   C; (*operating from 21 bases*)

25   F; (*The flying doctors and nurses serve more than a quarter of a million people*)

26   C; (*The effectiveness of the Flying Doctor is in its wide reach*)

27   A; (*also fitted out as flying intensive care units*)

28   F; (*its operations are funded by Commonwealth and State governments, public donations and corporate sponsorships.*)

READING PASSAGE 3

29   vii; (*But bit by bit, whale corpses are giving up their secrets.*)

30   x; (*locals immediately blamed the armed forces.*)

31   i; (*First, the noise can surprise the animal ... Second, soundwaves can themselves make bubbles with an effect very similar to that of compression sickness.*)

32   vi; (*Some whale species, it appears, are just too friendly for their own good.*)

33   ii; (*all mass stranding sites around Australia were gently sloping sandy beaches*)

34   xi; (*Rough weather generates more bubbles than usual and during and after a storm whales may essentially be swimming blind.*)

35   iv; (*major climatic cycles, years in which there are strong westerly and southerly winds that bring cool, nutrient-rich water*)

36   v; (*Some wonder why many whales, once rescued from the beach, turn around and beach themselves once more. One possible explanation may lie in the harm the first beaching does.*)

37   B; (*the noise can surprise the animal, causing it to swim too quickly to the surface, resulting in compression sickness (known to human divers as 'the bends').*)

38   C; (*whales have been stranding for a very long time – pre-sonar. So it can't be just that.*)

39   D; (*sandy beaches disrupt their echolocation system*)

40   A; (*There seems to be some anecdotal evidence in favour of James' storm theory. Strandings in Tasmania often occur in quite wild weather.*)

WRITING

Writing Test 1

Sample responses

Task 1

This bar chart shows that causes of stress change at different periods in people's lives in Canada.

Working too much is identified as the number one cause of stress by 27% of Canadians in the age group 25 to 54 and by around 15% of those aged 55–64. This is in stark contrast to the group of people aged 65–74 and 75 and above, of whom only 2% and 1% respectively rate it as the major source of stress.

Health problems increase as a stress factor as people get older: it is the main cause of stress of just 3% of the youngest age group, but 23% of the oldest age group. The opposite is the case with not having enough money, which falls from 15% to around 4%.

'No particular reason' is by far the number one cause of stress (more than 30%) for those aged 65 and over.

It can be said overall that as people in Canada get older, some sources of stress such as health increase in importance, whereas others such as lack of money and working too much become less important.

NOTES

The first paragraph makes a brief statement about the information contained in the bar chart, the following three paragraphs give data on the four main causes of stress and the final paragraph gives an overview. There would not be enough time to describe everything in the chart, but the main points have been mentioned and some comparisons have been made.

This essay has been structured by focusing on each cause of stress separately, but it would be possible to structure the essay differently; for example, by looking at each age group separately. There is also a range of vocabulary. *Cause of stress* has been paraphrased as *source of stress* and *stress factor; age groups* is also expressed as *in the age group 25 to 54, those aged 55–64, the group of people aged 65–74, the youngest group, the oldest age group* and *those aged 65 and over.* The present tense has been used throughout and there is some use of the passive; for example, *is identified as* and *it can be said.*

There are 187 words.

Task 2

The rapid development of communications technology has had a significant impact on society. There are both positive and negative sides to this, but the problem lies in the way this technology is used rather than in the technology itself.

Mobile phones and email make it possible to contact a person even when you do not know where they are. This allows for greater flexibility in people's lives, which opens up opportunities for individuals and for society. Families and friends can chat or write to each other anywhere on the planet at little or no cost. In addition, a mobile phone can be used to get help immediately and save someone's life in an emergency.

A downside is that some people have become addicted to their screens. While spending time with other people, they continually send texts on their mobile phones or are focused on their laptop computers and so do not give their full attention to the people around them. A text message or email is often superficial, unlike the potentially more genuine and personal nature of face-to-face communication. Some people may come to feel more comfortable communicating through devices rather than by talking to a person next to them.

The immediacy of this technology has also increased the pace of life and invaded people's privacy. A quick response is expected to an email and you may never be free of the demands of an employer, so that you may have less time to relax. Some people may even invent multiple identities online, which can be used to deceive others.

Modern technology clearly brings both advantages and disadvantages for society, so it is up to people to use it to their own benefit and to help society rather than to be enslaved by technology.

Writing Test 2

Sample responses

Task 1

These two line graphs show that since 1958 there has been fall in the percentage of the Australian population who are children, and that the percentages of children and young people are projected to decrease between now and 2038. However, their numbers have grown since 1958 and are expected to continue to rise until 2038.

The percentage of children aged 0–14 has fallen from a high point of 30% in 1958,

and it is projected that it will continue to fall gradually to around 17% in 2038. In contrast, the proportion of 15 to 24-year-olds rose to approximately 17% in 1980, but has fallen gradually since then. It is forecast that this group will make up just 12% of the total Australian population by the end of the 80-year period covered by the graphs.

However, the number of children and young people has increased since 1958, except for a short-lived slight drop. By 2038 it is expected that there will be a total of 5.2 million children and 3.7 million young people in Australia.

Overall it can be seen that the Australian population has aged since 1958 and that this process is expected to continue into the future.

Task 2

As many large cities around the world become increasingly crowded and polluted, imposing a charge on cars that enter city centres is an attractive idea. Although it does have some drawbacks, I support this proposal, though with some reservations.

Making drivers pay a fee to drive into the centre of the city would discourage some drivers, which would reduce the amount of traffic congestion as well as air pollution. Public buses and trams would then be able to get to their destinations faster, so commuters would not spend so much time travelling to and from work. City centres would be more pleasant places for workers, shoppers, cyclists and pedestrians in general.

It can be argued that this policy would discriminate against those who are less well off, because wealthy drivers would not be deterred by such a fee. Also, if the government failed to invest more money in public transport, travel by bus or tram could become more uncomfortable for the greater number of passengers. On top of that, it could be logistically and technically very difficult to install the equipment needed at the many points at which cars could enter the city centre.

I think that this policy is a good idea, though the fee on cars would not necessarily have to be enforced on weekends or late at night. This policy has the potential to make city centres more accessible for the general public provided that there was an efficient public transport system that was a viable alternative to the private car.

Overall, this policy is worth trying in order to reduce the domination of city centres by motor vehicles and to create a cleaner and more attractive urban environment.

NOTES
The first paragraph makes some introductory remarks about the topic and presents the writer's opinion. The second paragraph contains some arguments in favour of the policy and the following paragraph gives some arguments against it. The fourth paragraph restates the writer's opinion and the final paragraph is a brief conclusion.

Linking devices and signposting include *also*, *on top of that*, *though* and *overall*. *Pay a fee* is paraphrased as *impose a charge*, and less common words used include *reservations, commuters, deterred, logistically, accessible* and *viable*. There is a range of complex sentences and, as the writer is imagining the impact of the introduction of this policy, many constructions with *would* and *could* have been used.
There are 282 words.

Writing Test 3
Sample responses
Task 1
This diagram shows how electricity can be generated using the heat contained in the underground water that is found between layers of hot rock.

First, the hot water is pumped to the surface. It then passes through a heat exchanger, which extracts the heat from the water. This heat is used to run the power station in order to generate electricity. The electricity is sent by cables to the national electricity grid to become part of the electricity supply.

When the heat is extracted from the water, the water becomes cool. This cooled water is then pumped back underground through a second pipe. When this cool water reaches the underground water it is again heated up and the cycle starts again.

In summary, this diagram demonstrates how geothermal energy can be a renewable source of electricity, which takes hot water from underground and then later pumps it back underground to continue the process.

NOTES
The first paragraph makes a general statement about what the diagram shows. The second and third paragraphs describe the process, and the final paragraph makes a general statement.
Sequencing is shown through the use of *first, then, again* and *when*. As this

diagram describes a process, the simple present tense is used throughout and the passive voice is used frequently.

There are 153 words.

Task 2

The Internet has grown rapidly over the past two decades and it has come to play a central role in education, the economy and as a source of information on almost anything. It has evolved from a luxury to a necessity in many countries. For this reason, governments should take steps to ensure that anyone who wants to use the Internet can do so, otherwise the gap between the rich and the poor within societies and between developing and economically advanced nations is likely to grow wider.

First of all, accessing the Internet requires a computer or a more expensive type of mobile phone, as well as a telephone line or wireless connection. All of these cost money, and therefore can be obstacles that could prevent people going online. Children whose families lack the necessary equipment and connections at home are at a disadvantage compared to children whose families do. This does not mean that governments would be required to cover the cost of everyone using the Internet from home, but these facilities could be provided free of charge at school libraries and public libraries, especially for educational purposes.

Likewise, workplaces that do not have Internet access could lag behind workplaces that do. In poorer countries, governments could subsidise the purchase of the equipment and the provision of the infrastructure so that people can visit Internet sites and download information quickly and reliably, and thereby be better able to compete in the national and global economy.

Services and utilities such as running water, garbage collection and electricity were initially luxuries that became necessities. In the same way, as Internet access increasingly becomes a necessity for functioning in the modern world, it will be up to governments to make sure that their citizens have free or cheap access to it.

NOTES

The first paragraph contains some general comments about the Internet and presents the writer's opinion. The second paragraph outlines some of the costs associated with accessing the Internet and its importance in education. The third paragraph proposes why governments should help provide Internet access, and the final paragraph concludes the argument.

Cohesive devices include *first of all, for this reason, likewise, thereby* and *in the same way. Using the Interne*t is paraphrased as *going online, computers and an Internet connection* as *the necessary equipment and connections* and *these facilities.* There is a range of complex sentences.

There is a total of 299 words.

Writing Test 4

Sample responses

Task 1

This table shows that the rate of savings over this 18-year period was the greatest in Singapore and China, and that the lowest savings rate was in the United States.

Singapore had the highest rate of savings as a percentage of GDP in both 1990 and 2000, when it stood at 43.6% and 46.9% respectively. However, it was overtaken by China in 2008, where the savings rate came to 53.2%. In contrast, the United States had the lowest rate of savings in each year, with just 12.1% in 2008.

The only other two countries in which the rate of savings fell with time were Italy, where it dropped slightly from 20.8% to 20.6% in 2000 before falling further to 18.2% in 2008, and South Korea, where it went from 37.7% to 33.6% and finally 31.9%. India recorded a big increase from 2000 to 2008, while Germany's savings rate fell before returning to just above its initial rate by 2008.

This table shows that there were big differences between the savings rates in these seven countries, with Asian nations having higher rates than all the non-Asian countries in 2000 and 2008.

Task 2

Laws to prevent animals being used as entertainment are important in countries where animals are often not kept in suitable circumstances. If they are not fed properly or are mistreated, especially wild animals, they can suffer. In other countries, however, the rules protecting animals are quite strict. The animals do not come to any harm and, in fact, are given adequate food and may even enjoy their training.

Where a wild animal such as a lion or tiger is kept in cages all its life, it will almost certainly suffer stress and will show this by walking to and fro for hours in its cage. Since a circus must constantly be on the move, the creature will be confined like this for most of its life. Furthermore, training a wild beast to do something that is not natural is difficult, and an animal such as a lion or tiger might be unwilling to cooperate and consequently will be harshly punished for not doing something that it would not do instinctively.

The situation with domesticated animals such as dogs or horses is quite different. If the circus feeds such creatures their natural food and gives them the freedom that they would get normally working with humans, then I do not see anything wrong, particularly if the local government insists on regulations that protect the circus performers. If the creatures are well looked after and practise their tricks with a careful trainer, they might easily get to like their circus life.

In conclusion, it depends on the nature of the animal and the conditions in which it is kept. People should consider the best interests of the different animals rather than just their own wish to be entertained.

SPEAKING
Sample speaking tests

The following is an analysis of the performance of the three candidates in the sample speaking test on pages 100–13.

Assessment of Candidate 1

Fluency and coherence

This candidate occasionally spoke fluently, but overall the pace was too slow and he hesitated frequently. Some pauses before answering were too long. His delivery was not smooth and far too often he filled pauses with 'er' while thinking of the next word he wanted to say. This was particularly noticeable during the long presentation in the second part of the test, but occurred throughout the interview. Using such fillers as a technique to gain thinking time is part of normal speech, but if overused, they disturb the flow of conversation. He did not use the full minute that candidates are given to prepare their long presentation, and started to speak after about 15 seconds. Due to his slow pace, and with the pauses and hesitations, during the long presentation he was not able to say very much. Overall, he made very few long utterances.

Throughout the interview he clearly understood and gave coherent answers to the questions, though there were a couple of exceptions. When asked 'How do people usually find a place to live in your country?', he answered, 'The people, er, find, a quiet place to live in my country because the centre is so crowded and so noisy'. On a number of occasions when he had not understood a question, he asked for it to be repeated, which is quite acceptable in the test. Repeating or rephrasing words used by the other person is a way to get thinking time, or to ask for clarification and maintain coherence. When asked about places that 'are more pleasant to live in', he simply and correctly asked 'More?' However, he seldom echoed or rephrased words from the questions, apart from when he was asked about 'other factors' and he responded, 'I think main factor is …' He incorrectly echoed the examiner when he was asked 'what do you think are the healthiest drinks?' and he replied, 'I like healthiest drinks'.

Vocabulary

The candidate generally used vocabulary appropriately, but displayed only a limited range. On one of the few occasions when he used a less common word, it was used incorrectly: he talked of 'metropole cities' instead of 'metropolitan cities'. He said, 'my first degree is economy' instead of 'Economics', and 'I have to learn to economy news' instead of 'I have to keep up with news about the economy'. Particularly in giving information about himself, he should make sure that he uses the correct terminology.

Throughout the interview he used the word 'yeah', whereas 'yes' would be more appropriate for a formal speaking test. Some other examples of vocabulary used wrongly were when he referred to 'some celebrates' instead of 'celebrations' or when he said 'we have no residence areas', 'it has a high level of alcohol inside' instead of 'it contains a high level of alcohol', 'go by walking' instead of 'go on foot' or 'walk', 'we have a good relation in our apartments' (though later he correctly mentions 'relationships') and 'I can see a ocean or river or like this, or lake' instead of 'or something like this, or a lake'. He used 'very', 'little' and 'quite' as qualifiers, but said 'it's too different' instead of it's very different'.

Grammar

It is generally possible to understand what this candidate meant throughout the interview, even when he made errors, and there were many instances of grammar being used correctly. In some cases he corrected himself, for instance: 'and it's, er, it has, our home, flat has three rooms', 'you must', er, moving, eh you can be moved'. However, there were very few complex sentences and, as with vocabulary, there was an insufficient range of grammatical structures.

The simple present tense was almost the only tense used. On a few occasions he left out 'are', ('gossip magazines popular in my country', 'the people interested in this gossip or sport'), or else used 'is' instead of 'are' with a plural noun ('in my country is most popular drinks special Turkish drinks', 'the people is elite people', 'our home prices is not, er, high'). He generally used the final -s when necessary except when he said, 'my mum actually like the huge kitchen'. He also used the wrong verb: 'I don't interested gossip'. In one case the continuous form was used instead of the simple present: 'we talking to neighbours always' and the simple instead of the continuous: 'That's why I study English'. When it was necessary to use the simple past passive, it was done incorrectly: 'this building, this apartments, er, built several years ago'. On two occasions the -ing form was used instead of the infinitive: 'if you rent a house you can, er, you must, er, moving', 'prefer to buying a home'.

The plural forms of nouns were generally used correctly, but there were some exceptions: 'lots of facility', 'in Istanbul the people generally live in the apartment', 'there are lots of advantage or disadvantage', 'our neighbours also is kind peoples'. There were cases where the wrong preposition was used ('IT is related about information', 'this apartment's a little far to centre', 'this is other factor for choose their apartment', 'when I look at [out] the window'), or a preposition was used where it was not needed ('that's why the people prefer to magazines', 'the people prefer to quiet place'), or where the preposition was omitted ('the disadvantages own the house', 'always you live the same place').

Articles were mostly used correctly, but sometimes they were omitted: 'we lived in, er, seventh floor', 'I think main factor is, er, their jobs', 'it's advantage for make a good relationships'. Also, a couple of pronouns were omitted: 'I don't read [them] often', 'people prefer to drink [it]'.

Among other grammatical errors, there was one example of an incomplete comparative ('high quality than the others'); incorrect word order with adverbs ('you can get easily a friend', 'you can get easily a home'); the wrong word order with adjectives ('I, er, wants to live a, er, good view, has a good view apartments'); and an error in use of the negative ('if you live in the houses, er, you have, er, not a good relationships there for their neighbours').

Pronunciation

Generally, this candidate's pronunciation was clear, though it would have helped if he spoke a bit more loudly so that the listener did not need to strain to understand him. There were problems with some sounds (e.g. 'th'), and some words (e.g. 'metropole cities' and 'huge'). Word and sentence stress was good, as was linking (e.g. 'has a high level of alcohol inside', 'if you rent a house, you can'), although the overuse of fillers disrupted the linking of words. The slow pace, pauses and the frequent use of 'er' produced an uneven rhythm of speech.

Overall

The level of this candidate's spoken English is not yet high enough for study at university in an English-speaking country. He is relaxed, perhaps too relaxed, and needs to make his delivery smoother, faster, more coherent and more accurate. His level of self-correction makes him hard to understand and affects his fluency, coherence and accuracy. He needs to work on his accuracy in order to reduce this level of self-correction, and thereby improve his fluency. It would be useful for him to listen to many types of spoken English and to engage in conversation on a range of topics with different people.

Assessment of Candidate 2

Fluency and coherence

This candidate always responded promptly, giving detailed answers and engaging well with the examiner throughout, creating the impression from the beginning of the interview that she was speaking fluently. She was forthcoming and produced a lot of long utterances. When asked 'Why did you decide to do a Masters of Commerce?', she answered, 'Um, because I think, if I can gain the Master degree maybe I will give a good job in China. And I will have a more opportunity to get a good pay job which is more appealing'. When asked 'What are the most popular drinks in your country?', she answered, 'Beer, yeah … And, er, maybe Coca-Cola, but I dislike it. I always drink the orangey water and, uh, just drink the water'. Unlike the male candidate, she used the full minute to prepare her long presentation, and spoke more coherently and logically in that section of the test.

She made good use of words and expressions such as 'however' and 'of course'. When she did not understand a question, she asked 'Sorry?' or else repeated the word the examiner had used which she had not understood: 'Toward?', 'Treat?' She also established coherence by rephrasing words used by the examiner. When asked 'What factors do you think determine where people choose to live?', she said, 'I think most of … most of the important reason'. On a couple of occasions she did not answer the question, such as her incoherent response when asked about healthy drinks.

Vocabulary

In general, the vocabulary and expressions she used were appropriate although she lacked some basic vocabulary (for example, she used 'parking room' for 'garage'). However, her vocabulary range is often quite limited. She confused 'few' and 'little' when she said 'I have little friend', and several times used adjectives instead of nouns ('the important reason is comfortable and the price and the convenient') and nouns instead of adjectives ('the life is very leisure'). She is clearly a person who likes to communicate and was able to paraphrase to express what she wanted to say, though she rarely used idioms and the only less common expression she used was 'in a word'. She needs to find alternative ways to say 'I think' to express her opinions and to use more qualifiers than 'very' and 'quite'. Overall the range and level of vocabulary was simple.

Grammar

This candidate made a lot of basic errors, particularly with verb tenses and the use of the plural. Students with her level of English usually have studied the rules of the English tense system, but have problems using verbs correctly. She was generally good with the third person singular, yet often mixed confused tenses: 'I will going to have the Master of Commerce', 'If I have rent a house and I lived it for a, for a long time maybe I think oh it's OK to me, but when I look, um, with it to my friend maybe I will find out that his house is better to me, so I will all think maybe I will have to looking for another house'. She sometimes used the wrong verbs: 'I have the language courses in my college', 'the house has in Willoughby'. She needs to use the simple past tense more often: 'when I first came to Sydney' instead of 'once I have been to Sydney', and 'when I in China I live in the apartment'. The -ing form was sometimes omitted or misused: 'I will not spend a lot of time to see the magazine', 'instead of go outside', 'want to looking for a house'. She had trouble using conditional, hypothetical structures: 'If

I have my own house I lived in it and I feel oh that it, that belongs to me. And I think I have a family, um, but if I live in the house just rent from somebody, I think I'm always worried'. However, she did better later in the interview: 'If you want to go out or go to work, go to university, you'll find that the traffic always block, it will waste a lot of time'.

She often used the singular form of nouns rather than plurals: 'magazine', 'movie star, TV star and the singer, the famous singer', 'one of the reason', 'six bedroom', 'one of the problem', 'sometime they can find the insect climbing to my house. I'm afraid of it'.

But sometimes she used plurals correctly: 'and in other big cities'. As often happens with people whose first language does not use articles, she sometimes used them when they were not necessary: 'a lot of younger people like to see the magazine about it'.

The pronoun object was left out at times. When asked 'Are there any hot drinks you like?', she replied: 'No I don't like'; also 'they cannot control'. Some errors were also made with prepositions: 'study is better to me', 'not good enough to me' and the very common error 'most of people'.

She was quick to correct herself, such as when she said, 'such as beer or alcohol, alcohol water. Yeah alcohol drink, sorry'. In fact, she should have used the adjective 'alcoholic', but she was clearly monitoring her own words. Overall she showed a limited range of grammatical structures, though her errors seldom led to the listener misunderstanding what she meant.

Pronunciation

This candidate spoke in a loud, clear voice throughout the interview. There were mispronunciations, especially of sounds that are typically difficult for speakers of her first language, such as 'Macquarie'. She had difficulty with the pronunciation of some high-frequency words and expressions such as 'good pay job', 'college', 'which', 'high' and 'chat'. Often she linked sounds well, as with: 'I will continue my studies throughout my life' and 'it's very easy for you to go out for shopping'. She stressed the important words in sentences: 'maybe I will give a good job in China', 'maybe the *environment* is not good enough'. Yet she needs to use more weak forms. In some utterances, each word was given equal stress: 'you can gain some information about the magazine', 'but I dislike it', 'when I live in it' and 'most of people prefer to live in his own house because the rent of the house is quite expensive'. Her intonation is influenced by her native language, and although at times she uses stress timing and intonation to good effect, overall she uses non-standard intonation patterns that affect how she conveys meaning.

Overall

This candidate is an effective speaker but her spoken English level is not adequate for university level study. Although she seems quite fluent, her vocabulary range is limited to basic words and phrases, and her control of accurate grammatical structures is weak. Outside familiar topics she begins to lose the precision to explain what she really means. She needs to improve her accuracy, to expand her vocabulary into more precise terms that better express her meaning, and to use sentence stress and intonation more effectively. She may benefit by slightly slowing down the pace of her delivery to give a more considered response.

Assessment of Candidate 3

Fluency and coherence

As a fluent communicator, this candidate readily and confidently answers questions and expresses opinions, and generally responds appropriately and at length. He occasionally corrects himself, which is common in spoken language and quite acceptable in the test. There are few hesitations and they are mostly not long. If anything, the pace was too fast and speech would be more coherent if he spoke more slowly. Though he did make full use of the minute to prepare his long presentation, he would benefit from taking more time to think about what he is going to say.

His speech is generally coherent, though this does break down at times, particularly with a tendency to overuse some connectives, and to sometimes use them inappropriately. This can be seen especially with his use of the word 'so' at the beginning of utterances. For example, when asked which kinds of magazines are popular in his country, he responds, 'So in India people love cricket so the ...' and in the long turn when he says, 'So I love gardening also so I had a lot of flowers and er whether you sit at my place some home gardens. So the house was my favourite house in my whole life er until now. So I am still looking for a house for that kind of house. So because I want to live in a very peaceful area ...'. He also overuses 'also' when he says, 'they can use the internet also, it is really helpful. So you can do it at home also you don't have to go and see someone else so you can find it very easily on the internet also'. There is also a tendency to overuse the filler 'like', which is commonly used in informal language: 'Er in books like people have to spend a lot of time to get a idea what they reading about but in magazines they can get like er, er they can get an idea about the thing what they are reading about just in a shorter um period, short period of time and in a sense like short look, quick look, yeah.'

In addition, he overuses the conjunction 'and', for example, 'so these people are really helpful and they can find whatever they are looking for that's easy for them because they can tell them those people like what they are looking for and they will help to find those places and even on the other hand they can use the internet also, it is really helpful. So you can do it at home also you don't have to go and see someone else ...'. On occasion what he is referring to is unclear, for instance when he says, 'I want to do that nursing course' and 'it tells about those other products'.

Vocabulary

This candidate's range of vocabulary is adequate to convey what he wants to say, and he uses a number of idiomatic and less common lexical items appropriately. Examples are when he says, 'I'm really into like um looking after people', 'veggies', and with collocations such as 'homemade alcohol', 'separate toilet', 'dark chocolate' and 'basic needs'. He appears to be more comfortable in the use of less formal language (exceptions are when he says 'dispensaries' and 'congested').

In general his vocabulary lacks flexibility and precision, and he has a limited capacity to paraphrase. He makes some inappropriate choices when he says 'street view' instead of 'view of the street', 'migrant peoples' instead of 'migrants', 'colour wise and picture wise and the furniture wise', and 'line of poverty'. There is sometimes confusion between adjectives, nouns and adverbs e.g. 'the government financial', 'when I firstly came to Australia', and 'suburban is more wider than city'.

Grammar

This candidate produces complex sentences, though these frequently contain errors, e.g. 'if you are living in a house you have a separate wall from your neighbours or you will have a gap between your house and the neighbour's house, so you can't hear the neighbour's cry so it will be more separate from the – from other houses' … and 'in some like in developing countries the government should help those people who can't afford to buy a place um like um mostly those people who are living below the line, the line of poverty, so government should help them to buy a place'. There are also numerous errors with basic grammar, including with articles, tenses and prepositions.

Often the wrong tense is used, for instance when describing a place where he used to live he says, 'I like that because there is a park on the next side of the street. So I can watch people playing football because I love football and er it was near to all the facilities'. Also there are errors with the form of tenses, e.g. 'what they reading about' and ' you kind of feeling like'. This is also lack of agreement between subject and verb e.g. 'people who er owns their own home' and 'the curtains was really nice'.

There are numerous instances of errors in the use of comparatives e.g. 'more bigger than a apartment', 'more taller than a house ', 'some residential areas are very like er very good than others' and 'these kinds of places are very comfortable than others'. There are errors with articles, particularly omitting them: 'it's not

interesting subject', 'get a idea' and 'view of city'. The incorrect preposition is sometimes used e.g. 'near to', 'there is a park on the next side of the street' and 'on the wedding parties'.

Though what this candidate means is generally clear, there are several occasions when it is difficult to understand what he is trying to say. Instances of this are when he says, 'because uh in in this competition of us uh you need English if you are going it helps in your career', ' a house would be like very open side' and ' suburban is more wider than city'.

Pronunciation

Most of the time this candidate can be understood, yet his pronunciation would improve if he spoke more slowly. The main problems are at the level of sentences and phrases, where his intonation and rhythm sometimes make his message hard to comprehend, rather than with individual words. Meaning can be conveyed or made clearer through using pauses, yet there are insufficient pauses in this candidate's rapid-fire speech, and it is at times not immediately clear when he has finished responding to a question, e.g. due to him not using falling intonation.

Words are sometimes run together and the lack of chunking makes it difficult to tell when one idea has ended and another has begun. Some individual words and expressions are hard to understand, particularly due to a tendency to make long vowels into short vowels and through the wrong stress within words, e.g. with 'communicate', 'players', 'magazines', 'look', 'alcohol', 'peaceful', 'street', 'library', 'colour' and 'developing'.

Overall

Some people speak too slowly in the attempt to avoid errors and some have the opposite tendency. That is, they are so keen to communicate that they do not take enough care with accuracy. This candidate seems to belong to the latter group. He is adept at using colloquial vocabulary and has the confidence to communicate fluently, even if he sometimes lacks coherence. Overall, if he slowed down the pace at which he talks, he would have more time to think, which would mean he would not have to correct himself and change direction midway through sentences so often. This would also help him avoid some of the grammar mistakes, enable him to produce more coherent utterances, to use words such as 'yeah', 'so' and 'like' less often, and he would be easier to understand.

Audio CD contents

CD 1 Listening Tests 1 and 2		CD 2 Listening Tests 3 and 4		CD 3 Speaking Tests	
Track	**Listening Test 1**	**Track**	**Listening Test 3**	**Track**	**Speaking Tests**
1	Instructions	1	Instructions	1	Sample Speaking Test
2	Section 1	2	Section 1	2	Sample Speaking Test: Candidate 1
3	Section 2	3	Section 2		
4	Section 3	4	Section 3	3	Sample Speaking Test: Candidate 2
5	Section 4	5	Section 4		
				4	Sample Speaking Test: Candidate 3
Track	**Listening Test 2**	**Track**	**Listening Test 4**		
6	Instructions	6	Instructions	5	Speaking Test 1
7	Section 1	7	Section 1	6	Speaking Test 2
8	Section 2	8	Section 2	7	Speaking Test 3
9	Section 3	9	Section 3	8	Speaking Test 4
10	Section 4	10	Section 4	9	Speaking Test 5
				10	Speaking Test 6